MIND GPS

Navigation to Your Thriving Path

Amie Radzi

Copyright © ABLE Publishing Press
First published in Australia in 2025
by ABLE Publishing Press

Text Copyright © Amie Radzi 2025

All rights reserved. No part of this book may be used or reproduced by any means, graphic, electronic, or mechanical, including photocopying, recording, taping or by any information storage retrieval system without the written permission of the copyright owner except in the case of brief quotations embodied in critical articles and reviews.

Because of the dynamic nature of the Internet, any web addresses or links contained in this book may have changed since publication and may no longer be vaild. The views expressed in this work are solely those of the author and do not necessarily reflect the views of the publisher and the publisher hereby disclaims any responsibility for them.

 A catalogue record for this work is available from the National Library of Australia

National Library of Australia Catalogue-in-Publication data:
Mind GPS / Amie Radzi

ISBN:
978-1-922970-05-3
(Paperback)

Contents

Acknowledgement 1
Introduction: An Open Letter to You 3

Section 1: The Wake-Up Call - Know Yourself and Your Direction 5
Chapter 1: The Driver or The Passenger? Living Life in Default 7
Chapter 2: Your Direction and Destination 13
Chapter 3: The Pinpoint - Where are you now? 20

Section 2: The Roadblocks 27
Chapter 4: The Conditioned You 29
Chapter 5: Understand The Mind and Emotional States 35
Chapter 6: How to Thrive and Live the Life You're Meant For 45

Section 3: Your MIND GPS. Your Personalised Roadmap 55
Chapter 7: Your Growth 57
Chapter 8: Your Presence 63
Chapter 9: Your Self 74

Section 4: Mastering You and Become the Victorious Creator 85
Chapter 10: Mastering the Inner Game 87
Chapter 11: Becoming the Victorious Creator 95
Chapter 12: Envision Your Thriving Future 108
Chapter 13: Living Your True Potential 118
Chapter 14: Creating a Life of Impact and Meaning 127
Chapter 15: Impossible to I'm Possible 135

ACKNOWLEDGEMENT

To my parents — you are my everything.

To my dad: you are the reason I began and the reason I keep going.

To my mom: you are my rock, always steady, always there.

Without both of you, I would not be here, nor become who I am today.

To Abbey — you are my gravity, the one who grounds me and patiently walks with me through my dreams, my flaws, and my wildness.

To my family, coaches, mentors, teachers, brothers and sisters, friends, collaborators, clients, students, community, and every soul — even those who doubted me, challenged me, or crossed my path only for a moment. If I could name you all, this page would never end.

Please know this: I thank you, I appreciate you, I forgive you, and I am grateful for the role you have played in my life. Whether you lifted me up or tested me, you shaped me. In the end, my love and gratitude extend to you all, without exception.

Each of you lives in these pages, in ways seen and unseen.

And finally, to myself. Thank you for listening when silence felt easier. For rising again no matter how many times you fell. For moving forward through the highs and lows, when no one believed, when no one clapped, when no one saw, when no one understood, when no one stood with you. Yet you still rose. Thank you for continuing with love, humility, and courage. Thank you for turning your Mind GPS online, for trusting the journey, and so you can guide others too.

I love each and every one of you.

With deep gratitude, always.

INTRODUCTION
AN OPEN LETTER TO YOU

I don't know where you are right now,

Maybe you're tired … maybe you're hopeful…

Maybe you've been walking for so long, and you forgot why you started.

I trust this book will guide you from where you are, to where you truly meant to be.

In case you forget, or if no one's ever told you this, let me be the first to say:

You are not broken.

You are not behind.

You were simply shaped by a world that helped you forget who you truly are.

The world that taught you to *seek* your worth instead of *remember* it.

But within you has always lived something deeper.

Something more…

Something wiser … truer … lies within.

A voice. A vision. A knowing.

You may have silenced it.

Doubted it.

Even run away from it.
But it never left you.
You are not too late.
You are not too much.
You are enough.
This book was never about adding more to you.
It was a journey of returning.
A homecoming.
A renavigation back to your truth, your power and your purpose.
Now, *your* story begins.
Not the one you were told to live … but the one you were born to create.
So breathe in this moment.
You're no longer the passenger.
You are the driver.
You are your own compass.
You are your own North Star.
Your GPS has started to get online … and is now ready for a drive.
Go Live … Go Lead… and Go Love.
The world is waiting for your starlight.
You are exactly who you were always meant to be.
This is your moment. Go and live it.

Truly from my heart to yours,
Amie Radzi
Creator and Founder of Mind GPS

SECTION 1
THE WAKE-UP CALL - KNOW YOURSELF AND YOUR DIRECTION

Chapter 1
The Driver or The Passenger? Living Life in Default

'Before you can move forward, you must first wake up to where you are'

I used to live life in default; wake up by the alarm and get ready for work, drag myself out of bed, start the morning with coffee just to kickstart my body with caffeine - then rush to clock in at the job. Do the work. Drink more coffee for more energy. Clock out. Head straight to the next job. Eat whatever I could find just to fill an empty stomach. Get home, shower, collapse into bed, only to wake up and repeat it all over again. For me, the life I was living was just to pay the bills, work to support my living expenses, support my family and thinking I'd make life better *when I have more money.*

In 2008, while studying at college, I started a part-time job to earn some money for the little extras I wanted. My parents were still supporting me, but as an independent first child of four, I tended to go out and find ways to support myself. My intention was only to get money to have some freedom and independence. During that time, I thought we only ever had *just enough* and that made me want more – *just enough was not enough*. Seeing my parents struggle raising four of us, I realised I needed *to work hard* to get money. That was what I saw and all I knew. I learned that I must work hard to put food on the table, to pay the bills … and often it felt like a fight just to make ends meet. Since then, my life has been all about working - having two or three jobs at a time, doing anything I can to earn money. My college friend called me a 'workaholic.' After college, I would normally head to my part-time job, finish late at night or do a long weekend shift.

I actually enjoyed it! Back then I thought she had given me the coolest title – *Workaholic* - because I dedicated my life to working for the sake of building a better life. Going through many different success pathways back then, began with filing, store admin, working in a coffee chain and hospitality, marketing and sales in property development, personal assistant to a manager in the banking industry, event management, multi-level marketing and running businesses in multiple and a variety of areas; doing anything I could to earn money and *survive* in life. For eight years of searching, striving and building throughout that journey, it led me to one of the lowest moments in my life.

I hit rock bottom – hard! I was almost at the edge of bankruptcy from a failed business of mine, and my business partner. Abbey is a single mum with two children, who works really hard and is the breadwinner for her family. We both had the same values; building our lives to support and provide the best for our family. We decided to open a coffee shop together, building a business that is often seen as a success by others. After building the business for over two years, we had to shut it down - for so many reasons but mainly that we couldn't financially sustain the business.

MIND GPS

In 2017, I literally had no money to even eat. One day, I went to a grocery shop to buy some food. At the next counter, a friend who was also like a brother to us, saw us while we were about to make the payment. He smiled and he took out some cash - 50 Ringgit Malaysia – and gave it to the lady at the counter for all our items. He knew our situation and what we'd been through. We'd worked together for an event management group, organising Muay Thai State Events. I will never forget that moment - when I was at the lowest point in my life - yet someone was there to lend a helping hand. My heart is grateful to have kindhearted people like that in my life.

But what I truly felt in that moment was: *Why am I living this life, when I was supposed to be the one able to support others?* Week after week went by, finding a way to survive, day to day. One day, we took on a job cleaning an abandoned office. While in a low squat over the Asian style floor toilet, scrubbing away I said to Abbey. 'I can't believe we've had to stoop this low just to put food on the table.' As I turned back, I felt my eyes fill with tears. My heart was sobbing, holding the toilet bowl brush while reflecting on what I had to do just to earn some money.

The office owner offered us the work because he wanted to help us earn some money. Another person who was like a brother to us. I've always been lucky to have good people in my life. We just needed to find a job for our day-to-day survival. I carried so much shame with me, from having a failed business and being seen as a failure. For the next six months of regression, every day I would go to sleep late at night and not wake up till mid-afternoon … I just didn't feel like waking up. Life has its ups and downs, times with no direction. I was just going through the motions as a way to pay the bills and debts. I felt like my life was going nowhere. Every day, I woke up feeling there was no real reason to live; no work, no activities … just regret. It felt so dark. I am someone who is independent and wanting to build a life and I was at rock bottom after all my hard work. One day, I went to my mom's home, just to have some lunch to fill my empty stomach and, as I was walking out, I heard my brother say, 'you're just coming back home to eat, as you have no money to buy your own food.' I hold the vivid sounds and emotions from that moment deep in my memory. The moment I heard that, my world collapsed. It felt like my heart had been stabbed, and with a sharp deep pain, I felt no one else understood what I'd been through. He may not have meant it that way, but his simple words cut deep.

My mum, who's always there for me no matter what, will always say, 'come home whenever you want to, we are here for you.' As the eldest child, I really wanted to make them proud, and not burden them with my challenges. I would always stay strong in front of them, smile and just walk out, then cry when no one could see me. The shower was where my tears did not show but I was able to release all my feelings; a safe place where no one could see the sadness in my heart.

Choosing the Driver's Seat

One day, as she was scrolling Facebook, Abbey told me about our friend who was living in Australia. 'Maybe it's somewhere we can go to build a better life,' she mentioned. She spent some time searching and finding information, regularly talking to our friend about it. It took us over a year to make the decision because it's such a big thing to move and leave parents and family. For me, I had never been away from them, and for Abbey, she had to leave her two young kids with her mum, who was 62 years old at the time, while we were figuring things out. We were both so lost, but we needed to find a way to make things happen, to live our life and find solutions to our problems. So, in 2018, we made the decision to sell off what we had left from the cafe to earn to pay for flights and have a little money to survive.

With such a small amount of money on hand, we basically started from nothing to start building our life again. We had just $500 on hand for two people to begin a new life, flying to a place we'd never been before. It was a bold move but it seemed like the only real opportunity for us, while all the time feeling we were trying to breathe underwater.

Fast forward to around mid-year 2019, I was working at Starbucks Coffee in Brisbane. I was struck once again in menial job. While waiting for the oven to beep, serving food to customers, I was trying to catch my breath in an environment that never stops. As I turned back to the oven, something hit my mind - subtly but deeply: *Is this really how I am going to live my life for the next 10 years?* A deep self-reflection arose within. I was far away from my family but felt I was building the same life … again … with no purpose, just for the sake of working to pay bills. Life had become automatic; doing the same things, crushing my body, my mind and even my soul. *I'd had enough of all of this.* I didn't want to see myself in the same spot in the next ten years. I was losing time with my family. I was just working for the sake of it, wondering what I was chasing in life. I'd been waking up, not knowing what excites me, just going through the motions of life, like a robot. And once again, all I felt was *dread* - my body that pushing through life, each and every day, on default. At that point, fresh in my mind, I knew I wanted to make a difference, not only to myself, but for my family. That is the moment that woke me up; it was the starting point of *everything*.

I am sure in this life, people go through different pathways, with struggle and challenges, ups and downs, breakdown or breakthrough. I want you to know … life is only the way we see it through our own lens. The main thing is, whether you see it or not, *you and your life keep moving*. But the true question that hit me was: *Is this the life you want to live, and are you happy about it?* Are you in your comfort zone or truly happy with your life? For me, I felt there was something more in me. And this kept whispering, until I listened and decided to follow through.

At some point in life, many of us realise that we truly want to have a better life, doing and creating things, not only for ourselves and our loved ones, but for our community and humanity. We may not even be aware of how our life is driven by the things that are controlling us. No matter what it is, there is a driver in our life. I have learned through experience, that you must be *the driver* or you will be a passenger.

Science in our modern world, can now prove and, give real data to make it clear, that for 95% of our behaviour each day, it is the subconscious mind that drives us. The work of Bruce Lipton clearly explains this.

Being a driver means that you are the one who taking control of your life. Or will you allow someone else, or something else, to drive you while you just sit as the passenger? I made a decision in my life that no one is going to save me if I don't save myself.

And even if I want to save my family, friends and fellow people, I've got to start with 'me' first. No one else will, or can, do that for me. I am super grateful for the life that drove me and what I went through, which actually led me to something bigger and greater, something I wasn't even aware of. The journey is not easy but it is worth it. I want you to know how powerful it is when you decide to become the driver in your life and choose your own direction.

Truly, what I am sharing with you here, at the beginning of this book, is that no matter where you are in this life, even if you're in the middle of a challenging situation, what you learn will actually give you a beautiful gift to awaken your power. Now is the time! You can flip life in an instant, rather than become the victim or passenger in your story and journey. My story will be different to yours, but we are all on our journey to learn to live and create … by becoming the driver of our own destiny.

> *'Sometimes, where you are in life is redirecting where you are meant to be. Are you the driver or the passenger?'*

Chapter 2
Your Direction and Destination

'If you don't choose your path, the world will choose it for you.'

THE LIFE I WAS TOLD TO LIVE

Back in school, most of the time in the classroom, I would just sleep with my head on the desk while the teacher was speaking. I did enjoy computer class though, creating multimedia and designing; that was exciting for me. But what I was really into at school - was sport. I loved to be active in the field rather than sitting in a boring classroom. Whatever the sport, I was doing something I loved and enjoyed. I played all different sports; always being one of the first chosen in a team. I was also captain for the hockey and handball teams and even made it to the state-level selection for handball. I loved being out on the field, giving my best while playing. Perhaps because I was tall and strong, and a good team player - I'm not sure why. I remember in high school around the age of 14, two teams, from red and green faction, were fighting for me to be in their team -

that's how people wanted me on their team in school sports.

When I was 15, I would dream of becoming an athlete ... but my dad did not agree with my choices. He'd been a hockey player at the district level when he was at school and later played for the Armed Forces Service Corporation. He told me there would be no future for me in sports. 'Look how I am now,' he said. 'You're only hurting your body, and people will never appreciate you. It will never give you a good future.' I didn't understand at the time why he stopped me, and I became a bit of a rebel as a teenager. Now, I see that parents only ever want the best future for their children. I did continue to play sports at school but it was no longer something I pursued on a professional level.

High school finished for me in 2000, and I patiently waited for the result to decide what to do next with my future. I wanted to go to college and study Multimedia, as it was the only other thing that interested me. Once again, my parents both said, 'there is no future in multimedia. You must study something that will provide you with a good future. Being in an office could give you more of an opportunity.' At the time, and being Asian, everyone around me thought that working in an office was the pathway to building a successful life. Loving them both very much and chasing the success they wanted for my future, I enrolled in a Diploma in Office and Technology Management.

You can imagine ... the course was totally opposite to what I enjoyed. For three years, doing this course, I was not happy. But I did learn a lot along the way, and considering how I wasn't great at studying in school, I did well in college, finished within the time frame and got a good result. Graduating was a great achievement, especially considering it was for something I didn't enjoy. My work and life path at that time in my life was scattered, because I worked all sorts of jobs to earn money to survive.

While working in marketing and sales in property development, I was offered a better opportunity to work in office banking with the qualifications I had, and the funny part is, I did work as a Secretary to a

Regional Manager for four years. Though most people, just by looking at me, thought of me more as a security guard because of the way I looked and carried myself. (Even back in college, I was called into the college office because of how I dressed - it wasn't considered acceptable by the lecturers.)

THE SEARCH FOR MY TRUE PATH

Throughout many years of my journey, I was lost, walking down the wrong path - but I just kept going without realising it. Remember how I told you how I was programmed to chase money for security and safety in life? ... so I could support myself and my family? Well, going back to the 2019 story, when I decided I wanted to make a difference for myself, that's when I began to pursue *personal growth*. I started my self-development in 2019, with many different groups and legendary mentors, just following the whisper inside of me. It kept saying, 'follow your heart and let the path guide you'.

As part of my journey, I discovered I was lost and recognised what I'd been desiring and searching for most of my life. I started to see my passion, purpose and pathway again. It reminded me, that from when I was very young, whenever anyone asked what I wanted to do with my life, I'd reply by saying, 'I want to help people,' but I never really understood what that meant. Vividly, I remember playing with other kids at my auntie's house. I was sitting on a maroon couch and saying, 'I want to be a philanthropist when I grow up.' Strange words for a child, but I can still recall that moment so clearly. For years, I carried a desire to help people without knowing how it would take shape.

It wasn't until I was participating in a coaching session with the Jay Shetty Certification School, that it all became clear. And since 2019, I cannot thank myself enough, for the path I've been on that's led to where I am today. The choices I made from my mind visioning, my heart's desire and soul calling, has opened a pathway I could never have been taught by my parents or by those who surrounded me.

The Old Way vs The New Way
This is what I call *a traditional pathway*; one we have all been told is the *right* path:

- go to school
- then university or college
- get a good job
- get married
- buy a house
- have a family
- save your money for a good retirement.

Don't get me wrong, I never look at this as the *wrong* way, but truly, I don't feel that surviving or just existing in life is for me. Because I felt there was more in me. And, for me, this way of living is what I call - *The Old Way*. What I have experienced in life was all necessary for me to be where I am today. The difference is, I made the conscious decision and aligned my actions to become the driver in my life, and head in the direction and destination I have chosen.

If this is something resonating with you, you may have felt something speak straight to your heart and deeply to your soul. The question now is; *how can you be in the driver's seat and set a destination that is truest to you?*

Keep reading … and keep your mind and heart open.

Firstly, all you have to do is to make the decision that you will be the driver. Not just with logic, but with the true emotion of WHY you want to do this. What is it that YOU truly want to make for yourself and your family? We've been told for long enough that choosing something we want, is *selfish*. True … I will never debate with you about that. But if being selfish gives you meaning to make a difference to yourself or anyone around you – then that is never selfish.

Being selfish for a good reason, is *valuing yourself first - and loving yourself first.*

As Oprah Winfrey shared … '*You've got to fill your cup first, so that you have the inner resources to be of service to others.*'

Because when you choose you, you start to give yourself a love that you have forgotten to give. When I was younger, I was a people-pleaser. I was always doing something to make someone else happy, while I was shrinking down and lost.

Before you finish reading this book, I want you to see your life and journey as a beautiful gift that led to where you are today. The question I will leave you now is:

What is the right 'next-step' for you to take you where you want to go?

What is your destination? A place that calls *you* or someone else's destination?

No matter where you are right now, remember … it is truly the right place, right time, right moment to be in.

Before we close this chapter, I want to share a story that I believe will stir something in you. It is a story that is shared by author Bronnie Ware, a palliative nurse who cares for people in their final days. She relates that the most common thing people say when they are at the end of their lives, is, 'I wish I'd had the courage to live a life true to myself, not the life others expected of me.' This is their number one regret. It really crushed my heart, because I know how it felt to live a life of others' expectations, just going through the motions of life because you have to, or should do. These days, that is called living on 'Autopilot' – just like a robot.

For the past decade, in my job at a coffee shop and in hospitality, I meet over 100 people daily. I see and hear this 'autopilot' life from people who walk in every single day, buy a cup of coffee and through our conversations. People who go through the motions of life and crush their soul, for a job, without knowing their true reasons of living. As I was walking my own path to rediscovery, I came across a beautiful Japanese concept that spoke straight to my heart. It is called Ikigai, which means, 'Reason for Being.' Ikigai is about living your life with purpose, with four elements:

- *what you love*
- *what you're good at*
- *what the world needs; and*
- *what you can be paid for.*

I remember my coffee mentor mentioned to me, 'I am happy living in my ikigai.' That is where I first began to learn about Ikigai, where I truly understood about living a life that is meaningful, that gives you direction, fulfilling you from the inside out.

Research in psychology supports this idea. According to the Self-Determination Theory, people feel happiest and most alive when three needs are met:

- Autonomy - they are able to choose their own path
- Competence - feeling capable in making a decision and own it; and
- Relatedness - feeling connected to a bigger purpose related to self, a sense of belonging to what is truly yours.

Overall, it is not selfish to choose your direction and destination. It is, indeed, essential to your well-being and it can add longevity in life. A discovery began as a National Geographic expedition, in the five places around the world where people consistently live to be over 100 years old; these are called the Blue Zones. One of the common themes found, is knowing your sense of purpose; *knowing why I wake up in the morning'* adds extra years of life for a person.

MIND GPS

Let this moment be one where you stop defaulting and drifting, instead choosing your direction and destination, one that truly means something for you. Never look at the past with regret, but how you can empower and take control from here; make a difference to yourself and those around you.

> *'Sometimes every experience matters, even if you don't understand at the time. But later you'll realise they all played an important role in shaping your journey and who you become.'*

Chapter 3
The Pinpoint - Where are you now?

'No destination becomes real until you first know your true location.'

FOUND THE DESTINATION, BUT THE SIGNAL WAS LOST

I had the dream. The fire. The vision. Now, after over thirty years of living life, I am finally driving my own path. I have found myself again. I knew where I wanted to go and my destination ... but I just couldn't get there. Now, I'm driving a path that gives me fulfillment simply because I know where I'm heading. Even though the journey ahead isn't always clear, I wake up each day with a different energy; one fueled by passion and purpose.

Despite the challenge that I never really know what's in front of me, this is just how I want to wake up ... feeling greater than I used to. Since 2020, I have woken up 'excited' each and every day, knowing my purpose and passion, knowing where I am heading. I no longer dread going to a job without passion and purpose. The jobs I've had have become a steppingstone for my future. I have found myself building a passion business and helping others; and right now, I have found a life-coaching business that I want to get started with. I know what I want, even if I don't quite understand what it will take to get started.

Living in Australia, a new country after a big move and transition in life, I am making another decision, another transition on my path. Surviving in a new country as a migrant is never an easy thing; starting from scratch to build a life again, while juggling between jobs to support general living, and exploring self-study on understanding humans at a deeper level. This has been a passion of mine for a long time, and I've enrolled in course after course, program after program, event after event, all to help me run and build my coaching business. I've invested all my resources - time, money and energy – in the direction of the destination I am heading towards.

My destination is to have freedom in the life that I am able to build for myself and my family. I've never wanted to have a life that is stuck in a job just for the sake of earning money. I've had a dream since I was a young adult to sit on the beach with a laptop and have a job … anywhere and everywhere. Again, to dream is free right? I've never understood why all the dreams I have keep showing up, but now I know the dreams I have are all truly my heart's desire, mind vision and a self-calling, ready for me to create. Every piece of the puzzle in my journey I have collected as part of the bigger picture, after going through years of building my passion and purpose into the business I am creating.

I have evolved in my understanding. I realise how I kept circling in the same loops when I thought I was rising, but instead I was at the same place and nothing moved. Nothing changed. But what I was gaining was different strategies from different people. I still kept pushing myself hard, with two or three jobs to pay for all the programs I enrolled in, as well as to support myself living in a foreign country. For a while, I thought all those programs, courses, events, books and people would change my life. I was looking outside of myself for a solution … and yes, all of that added knowledge, and I learned a lot … but I was expecting those resources to change things. But they are all just tools in what I was learning and understanding.

On 12 July 2023, around 11.40am, while working at the coffee shop, I suddenly felt like something hit me on my back; it was an electric sharp pain. And I couldn't move; I couldn't bend my body, or even walk a step. I was alone at the time, with no one around. I took a seat. When a customer walked in, I forced a smile and battled through the pain, while walking slowly to serve them. I had no idea what was happening – the pain was indescribable.

For a few days after the incident, I was just lying on the floor, couldn't move; all I heard in the quiet morning was the clock ticking, birds chirping, I cried for being in an unbearable situation. The nights became sleepless with pain, and there was nothing I could do about it. I didn't go to the doctor; a part of me worried about the cost, but more than that, I kept telling myself I was strong and I'd be okay. That was always my mindset: still smiling and pushing through, telling myself I could handle it. It wasn't until a week later, when I still couldn't stand the pain, that I finally went to a physiotherapist. It was the winter flu season, and when I caught a fever, the coughing created even more pressure on my back. Each cough was a deep and painful hit. I wasn't only in physical pain, but because I couldn't work, the pain of not knowing how I would be able to survive financially with this condition was very stressful.

Life had forced me to stop … without my permission … and maybe that's exactly what I needed. I believe and trust that things happen for a greater reason. Being grateful in that situation taught me about trust and patience. It gave me time to reflect, rest and truly be. I became aware of all the ways I had pushed through in my life … with force. For almost two months, I wasn't fully able to work, but I forced myself to get some cash to support my living and pay my physio bills.

Within two months of reflecting on how I could 'make things happen,' I went to the gym to ensure I was taking care of my body, stretching and strengthening my core and lower back, with the exercises recommended by the physio. One day in the gym, sitting on the bench as I slowly did the exercises, music played and all my memories surfaced, reminding me how *I don't feel I am enough*. I kept chasing and doing things in life, purely because I wanted approval and love from my parents and others. True, I wanted to build a life, but all I was doing was pushing through, because I was thinking; *I am not enough*. Even in the business I was building, I was hiding behind the shadow of *not enough*, so I never *properly* showed up.

Instead, I kept learning and chasing because I didn't feel competent and confident.

Who am I to do all of this?

Do people accept me and listen to me?

Am I truly able to make a change if they pay me?

Secretly, I was playing this all in the back of my mind without realising it had taken control of my behaviour and actions. As I closed my eyes and felt the beat of the music for a moment, tears began falling down my cheeks. My body felt tense and I remember being paralysed by inaction. I wanted to share my business with others, but I kept making excuses for not making it happen. It was fear... I never understood why I was doing all I was doing, until these memories came to the surface to tell me why I was playing small and circling in the same loops.

Your Pinpoint Moment

Like any GPS, you can't find your route until you know your exact location. Your 'now' is not just your job title, income, or relationship status - it's the story you're living. It's the energy you wake up with. It's the truth behind your patterns, habits and emotions. Have you ever found yourself doing all the right things but still feeling stuck? Are you running toward your dreams, inspiring others and in the life you are meant for? Or are you circling in the same loops, always wishing for more?

Sometimes, we think we're moving forward but in reality, we're just running in circles because we haven't stopped to pinpoint where we really are – or where we're going.

Maybe your story is different to mine - but I do know one thing. Until you stop to look at where you truly are, and not just with material or physical evidence, but truly look in your heart, until then, the loop will keep repeating in all areas of your life; business, career, relationships, financial. This chapter is the mirror where you can stop pretending or performing. Start going deep to pinpoint the real you and the real situation you are in right now ... and do it with compassion not judgement.

The Science of Self-Awareness

In your brain, your prefrontal cortex is like your internal GPS, it monitors and reflects. But, when you are in autopilot or default mode, the default mode network takes over, replaying old patterns and stories. There is a huge amount of research which shows that mindful awareness and self-reflection activate the prefrontal cortex and interrupt the survival loops stored in the limbic brain. According to a study by Tasha Eurich, an organisational psychologist in Harvard Business Review, 95% of people believe they are self-aware, but only 10-15% actually are. Self-awareness is one of four components of emotional intelligence, which can be learned, developed and enhanced. People who are self-aware tend to be more confident, make better decisions and build stronger relationships.

For me, self-awareness is not about being perfect, it's about being honest. When you name your patterns, your fears, your truths, that's when transformation truly begins. Psychologists also talk about the concept of *emotional avoidance*. When we avoid uncomfortable feelings, we reinforce the same patterns that keep us stuck. But when we pause, reflect and feel like I did on that gym bench, we begin to shift the internal GPS.

Here is one of my favourite quotes by Carl Jung that I would love to share with you.

> 'Until you make the unconscious conscious, it will direct your life and you will call it fate.'

THE HONEST REFLECTION

This is the mirror - the honest reflection. Not the kind that tells you how good you look, but the kind that reflects what's really going on inside. A mirror doesn't lie. It just reflects what is there, whether you're ready to see it or not.

Throughout building this journey, I learned I was living an unhealthy, toxic positivity for most of my life, always telling myself everything was good, even when it wasn't. I smiled, pushed through, and wore my 'positive attitude' like armour. People even knew me for it. But deep down, I didn't realise what I was really doing: hiding even from myself by the illusion of being positive. That kind of positivity became a mask, and behind it was resentment, frustration, exhaustion and pain.

'I learned that toxic positivity was escaping my true feelings in a real situation, like when I said to myself, 'you are strong' just to make things look or feel better instead of allowing myself to simply be. Real positivity was different. It was facing the pain, challenges or situation honestly and still choosing to grow from them.'

One day, I realised that my 'positive' attitude was really a protection — a way of only seeing the good, while ignoring the other side. What I had to learn was to be neutral, to understand that everything has a reason. Not to hold on to positivity as a mask that blinds me, but to see both sides of life with clarity. Life kept reflecting back the truth I didn't want to see. Every struggle, every setback, every situation, every emotion was a feedback, a mirror showing me what was real. When I finally stopped pretending and looked honestly, the reflection wasn't there to destroy me, it was there to free me. This chapter is your mirror too; an honest reflection. *Are you being true to yourself or simply covering up to feel good?* What is it showing you right now? What are you pretending is fine when really it isn't?

I learned that denial is also a protection. It shields us from pain, but it also blinds us from the truth. And the truth is what really sets us free. If what you see is true for you, that's great, embrace it. But if it isn't, don't hide from it. Face it. Don't judge it. Just notice it. Because you can only rise above it. Your awareness is the seed, and it is where real freedom begins.

> '*The only way to shift your Mind GPS is to be radically honest about where you stand. That's how your real journey begins.*'

SECTION 2
THE ROADBLOCKS

Chapter 4
The Conditioned You

'Your past may shape who you are today, but it does not dictate who you are tomorrow.'

THE INHERITED BLUEPRINT

After three months of physical injury, my mental, emotional and physical state was in chaos; I had hit rock bottom - again. I felt exhausted and burned out, as if I'd been running through wall after wall. It felt like nothing was working for me. I worked hard … giving everything to always try to be and do the best I could. As I walked into my little home office, I threw my bag on the floor. I felt stressed, angry and frustrated after everything I did to work on my passion business for three years. I'd invested all my time, energy and money to the point of my deepest frustration. I screamed out loud in my mind: *What else can go wrong?* Looking back, I can see I was trapped in a victim mindset, reacting to life instead of navigating it. In that moment, I felt all the pain; physical, emotional, and mental. But the gift was that by letting myself feel it fully, I also found the strength to come back up. I sat at the table and cried, but no one saw my tears behind my smiling face and positive attitude. I'd done everything I could to build my business … but nothing seemed to work out. My heart was beating fast, my breathing hard, my chest visibly moving up and down … it reminded me how everything I did daily had led me to my physical injury … because I pushed through so hard … every day and night.

In that moment, I took my earbuds, put on some music, and allowed myself to feel the emotion come out. Listening to music from Andy Grammar, the lyrics hit me straight in the heart. When I'd almost given up on myself again - on my dreams, on my business, on the life that I am building – those lyrics about not giving up when it feels like there's nothing left, made me stop and rethink. One thing I've learned throughout my journey, is when you have passion and purpose, you will have persistence. These are the things that keep me going no matter how much I fall. Passion, purpose and persistence allow me to reroute back to the path I am on.

The roadblocks are there to test how deeply you want to live the life you are meant for. It is the beauty of the journey that makes you stronger and wiser. There are a lot of people who only share the destination, the celebration, the winning, the results … the outcome. But truly, only winning on this journey won't make me who I am or get me where I am today. It's the challenging times that build resilience and enable me to gain this gift that I am about to share with all of you here today. This is the same process for you. What I truly want you to see, feel, do and believe, is to embrace every journey you are on … before and after. It makes who you are yesterday, today and tomorrow.

Since I was young, I've always wondered why people do what they do; I've tried to understand human behaviour. This is the question that keeps me interested and curious. As I was going through my own experiences, wondering why I do what I do, I knew I wanted to build a life and passion business, but I didn't even understand why, or what, kept me going. Until the day when I listened to that music, and heard those lyrics, my mind had kept bringing memories to the surface; the same stories playing, the same behaviour circling - all from the tiredness of constantly pushing. That's when I realised there's a programme built into my operating system.

As mentioned earlier, Dr Bruce Lipton shares that 95% of our behaviour is driven by the subconscious mind; that our habits, reactions and beliefs all operate *below our awareness.* If you are stuck in the same mental and emotional pattern, you are running in the same program - and you may not even know. This is called the subconscious mind, which keeps replaying old patterns, behaviour and habits. *They are not just thoughts, they are programs.* From this moment, I realised I wasn't broken, I wasn't behind, I was just running on an outdated operating system that wasn't serving me well in my life. The program had been shaped by my past, my culture, my upbringing and my survival patterns.

The human operating system is what's been running in the background all your life; creating the beliefs, the reactions, fears, and habits that you didn't choose ... but inherited. Just like a phone comes with a default setting, so do we. But the wonderful truth is ... you CAN change it!

Your Human Operating System
Your human operating system is built through these 4E's, which I call - the Roots of Programming. This is your internal blueprint, formed through four major sources:

1. **Environment:** Everything around you when you were growing up - your home, culture, community, school, and the people you looked up to. It's what you saw, heard and felt before you even knew what was happening.
2. **Experience:** These are the things that keep happening over and over. Everything you've experienced and been through will shape you.

Things like how people reacted to you, what they praised you for or what they judged you on. All of this shaped how you see yourself today.

3. **Events:** Significant emotional moments that left a mark ... good or bad. These moments are sometimes celebrated, but other times silently stored. Even if you didn't talk about how you felt, your body remembered. Some moments stay with you, even when your mind forces you to forget.
4. **Epigenetics:** The generational patterns you were born into. Yes ... science now shows that trauma and resilience can be inherited. What didn't start with you may still live *in* you ... until it gets healed *through* you.

So, let's try to understand how our life *environments, experience, events* and *epigenetics* have shaped who we are, running our everyday life without us knowing it.

Since I was young, I saw my parents struggle, and work really hard, to raise us in the best way they could. My dad works as an Industrial Security Officer. My mum was always hustling; waking up early in the morning, rushing to the market for stock, then coming home to prepare the food that she would go out and sell in the small food stall in front of the house to support my dad. Her day always finished late into the night and she never relaxed until all the cleaning was done at home. On top of that, she added 'selling Tupperware' to earn more money to support my dad. In 2000, my dad was retrenched from a job, and suddenly he had no job and income. My dad also once had a joint venture business with his friend, selling watermelon and other fruits, as a side hustle, to earn enough to raise four children and support the family. With the cash he got from the retrenchment, they opened a small cybercafe in front of the house to help keep the family supported.

They went through a lot of hardship, often fighting, but of course, this is what I learned from. As a child who didn't understand adult life, *I absorbed what I saw through these environments, experiences, events and even carried the imprints of generational patterns passed down through epigenetics.* I was living through inherited experiences, carrying their stories and struggles, that weren't entirely mine, yet shaped the way I saw and navigated the world. It doesn't matter what emotions I felt through seeing and experiencing that environment and events, but what does matter, is the *meaning I gave it unconsciously.*

One day, I realised I was always working two or three jobs in a day, to help me feel secure. From what I'd seen, I had to work really hard to make ends meet, and I didn't want to *feel scarcity* like I'd felt growing up or have those experiences again. It was a behaviour that I never knew was silently playing and running on repeat, throughout my whole life. It became one of my blueprints running in my human operating system. These stories did not just shape my beliefs, they became the emotional codes in my body.

These Roots of Programming are built and saved as a memory in our brain and body. This root experience in life has stayed as a memory, according to Psychiatrist Dr Bessel Van Der Kolk, who shared in his work, *The Body Keeps The Score*, as a traumatic stress at the root of neuroscience. It is associated with the functional and chemical changes in the emotional part of the brain; the limbic area and brain stem. Dr. Joe Dispenza, international speaker, researcher, author and educator in neuroscience, epigenetics and quantum physics, says that by age seven, we've already built our subconscious identity. Most of our actions come from *habitual emotion + thought patterns.* Your body becomes addicted to the emotion of struggle, so even when you want freedom, your system brings you back to the familiar. Now, I would like to invite you to pause for a moment, just like I did on the day with the music playing.

- What patterns do you see and keep repeating in your life?

- Whose voice do you hear when you feel like you're not doing enough?
- What beliefs do you hold about your worth or success?

Sometimes it is playing silently or quietly, but it's so loud, it takes over your operating system. And just like GPS, once you update the system, everything starts to recalculate again. This is the beginning of your new direction, the start of seeing everything about yourself - your thoughts, your emotions, your beliefs, your mind and your system - with new eyes.

'Sometimes your history exists only to give meaning to the story you're meant to create.'

Chapter 5
Understand The Mind and Emotional States

'Your mind is not your enemy. But it can become your prison. Until you learn to listen, feel, and free it.'

I HAD THE COORDINATES, BUT NOT THE CONFIDENCE
I remember one day, I was sitting alone in my room at my desk, staring at the papers scattered in front of me. It felt like it was *everything* I'd been working on; all the ideas, all the effort, all the energy I poured into building my passion business. Suddenly, I felt it was just ... too much. I was overwhelmed; not by the work itself, but by the pressure within me. The weight of another moment where I felt like giving up ... again. Music has always been my companion, especially during times of reflection. That day, the song *Trustfall* by Pink came on. As the words rose about fear and desire, it felt like they were speaking to me directly. I felt a knot in my stomach. I realised - I was scared. Not just in my head, but in my whole body.

I was scared of failing. Scared of being seen. Scared of being judged. Scared of doing the wrong thing. And even more … scared that none of this would ever work. Fear has been with me for as long as I can remember, but I never noticed it until I started listening to it. It used to show up as hesitation, procrastination, inaction, self-doubt, perfectionism, burnout, or overthinking. It wore many masks. I didn't know it was fear. I thought it was just 'who I am.' All I ever wanted was to move forward, to live my purpose and do meaningful work. But I kept freezing and paralysing in action. I kept hearing that inner voice:

- What if this doesn't make sense?
- Who's going to listen to me?
- Who am I to call myself a coach, a speaker, or a teacher?

Even though I had real results, real transformations with real clients, my mind kept whispering that *I wasn't enough*. I'd had clients who found themselves again and built their dream passion business themselves. Clients who'd healed from deep-rooted experiences and reconnected with loved ones after years of disconnection because of the pain they'd been through. The anger and frustration that had sat with them had finally come back to heal with love. Clients who finally loved themselves again and started believing in themselves and their dreams.

I had witnessed all these beautiful shifts and changes in people's lives … and still, my mind kept looping the same old doubts. It was as if no amount of evidence could change the story running inside me. That's when I finally saw it:

My brain wasn't just thinking. It was protecting.

It was trying to keep me safe from judgement, rejection; from pain, from failure. But it was also keeping me stuck. I realised this wasn't about strategy anymore. It was about something deeper. I needed to understand my inner world, not just my thoughts, but the emotional states I was living in. That day, sitting in silence, I searched for the answers I needed to make myself better and move forward. I said to myself, 'I'm going to understand my mind, and I'm going to understand my emotions. Because I can't keep building my future on top of an unhealed foundation.'

The Mind Is Not Just Thought, It's A System

Most people think of the mind as just the thinking part; the voice in your head. But what I have found in my mind, is far more than that. It's not just mental, it's emotional, physical and spiritual. Spirituality is not about religion. (I'm not here to talk about religion). What I am here to share with you is, that spirituality is unseen, as a deeper meaning and connection with yourself first, and then to others and the world around you. Through years of personal study, in real life searching, and true-lived experiences, I discovered that the mind has layers and levels of consciousness, which each play a different role in how we live, act, think, feel and be. And once I began to see these layers clearly, I was finally able to understand why I kept looping in the same stories and emotional states.

7 Layers of the Mind

Awareness Level	Layer of Mind	What's Happening	What It Feels Like (Practical Examples)
Conscious	Thoughts	Self-talk, ideas, focus, daily choices. Shaped by how you perceive situations and the feelings you notice in the moment.	Clarity, presence, focus or autopilot, chaotic, overthinking, confusion.

Subconscious	Beliefs and Emotions	Beliefs, moods, and emotional memory shaping your responses.	Motivated, confident, trust yourself or feeling anxious, not good enough, stuck in old stories.
Subconscious to Unconscious	Nervous System Response	Body reacts when old patterns are triggered.	Calm in body and ability to pause or heart racing, tight chest, snapping, can't relax.
Unconscious (Surface)	Habits & Automatic Behaviour	Learned survival responses and routines (fight, flight, freeze, fawn)	Standing on your ground or taking quick action or avoiding, lashing out, shutting down, people pleasing.
Unconscious (Deep)	Memory & Conditioning	Old conditioning, suppressed wounds, repeated cycles.	Freedom when you release old stories or repeating mistakes, self-sabotage, avoiding discomfort.
Unconscious to Superconscious	Identity Layer	Sense of 'Who Am I?' and nervous system balance	Grounded and secure in yourself 'this is who I am' or doubting, comparing, confused identity.
Superconscious	Higher Mind / Core Self	Intuition, wisdom, vision and soul truth.	Connected, guided, inspired, creative or feeling lost, disconnected, chasing signs without clarity.

MIND GPS

The 7 Layers of the Mind is a model I've developed through years of learning, reflection, and lived experience. It isn't a scientific formula, but a practical map to help you see how your mind works on different levels. Psychology and neuroscience describe the conscious, subconscious, and unconscious mind, as well as a role of decision making, memory, habits, and the nervous system. Timeless wisdom also speak of higher awareness or the superconscious. What I've done is bring these ideas together into one simple model. This framework isn't about proving theory, it's about giving you a way to understand your own thoughts, emotions, and behaviour and to reconnect with your true self. Use it like GPS: a guide that helps you locate where you are, so you can choose where to go next. In simple terms, the *7 Layers of the Mind* represent the different level where our thoughts, emotions, habits, and memories live. Each layer affects us in its own way – some we notice, others run quietly in the background. Together, they shape how we think, feel, act, and live.

The 7 Layers of the Mind help you to see the details. The 4 Levels of Consciousness show you the bigger picture.

4 LEVELS OF CONSCIOUSNESS

Level	Awareness	Function
Conscious	Awareness (What you can see, think, feel, act and choose.)	Active awareness and decision-making.
Subconscious	Repetition	Learned habits and patterns
Unconscious	Protection	Hidden memories, roots and conditioning.
Superconscious	Guidance	Inner wisdom, intuition, and soul truth.

The *4 Levels of Consciousness* give you a big picture. While the *7 Layers of the Mind* zoom in on the details of how your mind works, the 4 Levels zoom out to show where your awareness is operating as a whole. Instead of analysing every part — thoughts, emotions, memory or the nervous system — this model asks a simpler question : 'What state of awareness am I in right now?'

- At the surface is the conscious, where you see the way you think, feel, act, decide, and focus on daily life.
- Just below is the subconscious, where beliefs, emotions, and habits quietly shape your choices.
- Deeper still is the unconscious, where old conditioning, memories, and survival responses are stored.
- At the highest point is the superconscious, your higher mind or true self — the place of intuition, vision, and soul truth.

These levels act like a lens. They reveal whether you're living from clarity, reacting from old patterns, running or hidden drives or guided by your true self or higher awareness. Simply recognising which level is leading you can change the way you think, feel, act and live. Understanding these levels helps you see why you sometimes feel in control and are at other times stuck. Awareness is the key; once you know which level is running the show, you can choose differently and navigate it.

Each layer and level communicates with the others. And until we become aware of what's happening beneath the surface, we keep living from outdated programming that no longer serves us. I'd like to share a quote I created, inspired by Carl Jung.

'*The meaning you give becomes the reason you repeat. Until you make the unconscious conscious, you will keep living the same pattern, just in different places, faces and phases.*'

MIND GPS

EMOTIONAL STATES: THE INVISIBLE ENERGY THAT DRIVES YOU

At the same time, I realised I wasn't just living in mental patterns, I was also living in emotional states. These weren't just feelings, they were frequencies; the vibration of emotions. I am sure you've heard about it; *emotion is equal to energy in motion.* But I never truly understood what it was until I lived through it. I did not realise it had played such a huge role in everyone's life. And as I have been in coffee shops and hospitality for over fifteen years, I see it every day, how people are driven by this – knowingly or unknowingly. People walking in, carrying their state with them - stressed, heavy, joyful, hopeful - and not even realising it. Whether you knew it or not, emotions were driving your choices, your tone of voice, even the way you walked. As a curious person wanting to know why people do what they do, I love to observe, study real life human behaviour and question why. Now, I was looking for the answer for myself, to help me to move forward. And this led me to be inspired by Dr. David R. Hawkins' Map of Consciousness. I began to understand that emotions carry measurable energy and that most of us live in the lower states … far more than we realise. That idea opened my eyes, but I wanted to make sense of it in my own life and language.

I began to see emotions as part of an energy spectrum. Some emotions are contractive states — they pull you down and make you small. These are the heavy emotions like shame, guilt, apathy, grief, fear, desire, anger and pride. They tighten the body and keep us stuck in survival.

Then there are transitional states - the turning points. These include courage, neutrality, willingness, acceptance and reason. They don't always feel easy, but they create momentum. They are like doors opening, helping you shift direction and recalibrate when you've gone off-course. Reason is powerful here, brings clarity and understanding, but it still lives in what I call *the mind's control zone*. You're trying to make sense, to manage, to figure things out. It stabilises you, but it can only take you so far.

Finally, there are expansive states — emotions that lift you higher and open you outward; love, joy, peace and enlightenment live here. These are *beyond the mind's zone*. They don't come from analysing or controlling, they come from opening. Here the grip control softens, and you step into flow, connection and freedom.

When I began to see emotions this way, I realised they weren't random feelings or moods but signals, feedback and messenger. A kind of inner compass inside me. Contractive states showed me when I was off-course. Transitional states helped me redirect and recalibrate. Expansive states confirmed I was aligned with my true path. This became part of how I began to navigate with my Mind GPS. I call this the Mind GPS : Emotional Energy Spectrum.

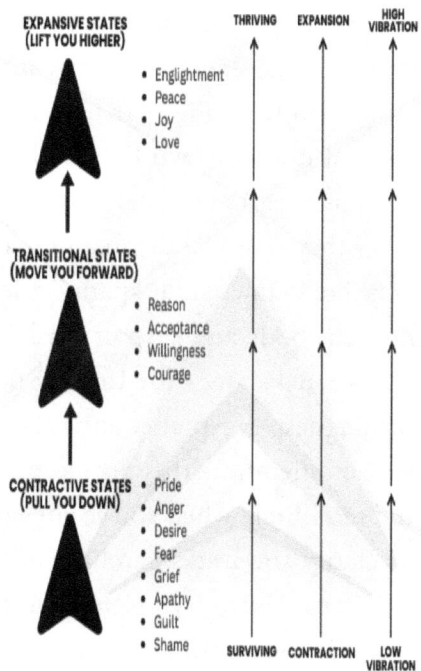

Mind Clicks

Ever since I was young, there has been one question that has always piqued my curiosity - '*Why do people do what they do?*' All of this now started to make sense and answered my longing question. Every time, every place, every person, every situation, I was driven by this one question … and finding a way to help people. The more I tried to help others, the more I lost myself. It wasn't until I gave up, and chose to help myself first, that everything started to change. When I looked at my life through this lens, I realised I had been living in fear for a long time in my life. And I never knew about it … even while chasing my dreams. No wonder I kept hitting walls. Those walls were there, wanting me to wake up and do things differently. Here is a model I created on *States of Living*, which we don't even realise we are operating from.

**THE 4 STATES OF LIVING :
FROM REACTION TO CREATION**

THRIVING

VICTORIOUS
CREATIVE

MASTER
"Life happens as me"

VICTORY
PROACTIVE

VICTOR
ACTIVE

MANIFESTOR
"Life happens through me"

VICTIM
REACTIVE

MAKER
"Life happens by me"

MASSES
"Life happens to me"

SURVIVING

The Turning Point

The day I chose to explore these inner layers was the day everything changed. I stopped blaming myself for being stuck. I stopped forcing, started listening and began creating. I stopped chasing and started feeling. And slowly, I began to reset … recalibrate … realign.

Reflection: Your Turning Point

You've now explored the models of operation and the stages that quietly shape every choice, feeling and result in your life.

But reading about them isn't the turning point - deciding to look inward is.

Take a few quiet moments with these questions:

1. Which state of living describes you most right now?
   - Reactive? Active? Proactive? Creative?
2. Which emotional vibrations run you most of the time?
   - Calm? Driven? Anxious? Hopeful?
3. Where in your life are you forcing ... and where are you listening?
4. If your inner GPS could speak, what destination would it tell you it's set to today?
5. What would you choose to recalibrate first? — Your focus, your energy, or your direction?

Be open. Be honest. This isn't about judgment - It's about awareness.

Self-awareness opens the door to self-regulation. Self-regulation leads to self-direction. And self-direction is how you *reset, recalibrate and realign* toward the life you actually want.

Your turning point begins here.

'The meaning you give creates the direction you live.'

Chapter 6
How to Thrive and Live the Life You're Meant For

'Thriving isn't something you chase or do. Thriving is something you Be and Become'

THE MIND THAT DRIVES YOU

We often hear the phrase, *Change your mindset, change your life*. But what if your mindset isn't just a conscious choice? What if it's actually a deeply wired operating system built from layers of mind. I have shared previously how you are operating subconsciously or even unconsciously. Your mind is not just a thinking machine. *It's a meaning-making, pattern-recognising, protection-seeking system.* It collects stories, forms identities, reacts to fear, and builds mental maps to help you survive. And over time, these maps become the very roads that keep you driving on autopilot, even when you long for a different destination.

Most people are trying to move forward while their internal GPS is set to the past. Most people are trying to build a new life while running on an outdated map. That was me; circling, driving and losing my true navigation.

When I first began exploring personal growth, I was focused on strategies, looking for 'How to' productivity hacks, goal-setting, vision boards ... all useful tools. But no matter how much I learned, something kept pulling me back. I would get stuck in cycles of overthinking, procrastination, fear and self-doubt. My thoughts were loud. My nervous system was constantly on edge. I didn't feel safe to take risks or to be fully seen. The conflicts inside were louder and stronger, and that made me confused about my direction.

It's not just about what you do, it's about what's driving what you do. We all have a reason why we want to do something, but we never see the reason *why we are not doing it.*

That's when I started to look under the hood. Not just *how* I think, but *why and why not*. My mentor once said, 'We see why we want to do it, and it's great. But why are you not doing it?' That opened up a deeper layer of understanding the mind. *What beliefs had I inherited?* What meaning was I attaching to failure, success, love, or visibility? Why did my body react with fear every time I wanted to step into something new? These weren't just random reactions - they were programmed responses. *And many of them weren't mine to begin with.* Our minds store meaning like files in a computer. But unlike a device, most of our 'files' weren't consciously created, they were installed without us even noticing. Just like cookies in a web browser, quietly saving bits of information while you browse, our minds collect experiences, beliefs and emotional imprints *in the background.* We don't always know they're there ... but they still influence what loads on our 'screen' every day. They were shaped by early experiences, modelled behaviours, traumas, cultural expectations, even generational patterns, passed down without question.

MIND GPS

THE PROGRAMS BENEATH YOUR POTENTIAL

I used to chase things in life, to try and create a better life. I thought thriving meant having more money, more success … more doing. But I was wrong! I was chasing something outside of me. I wanted to have a successful business that earns thousands in income, build a life of freedom, able to travel anywhere. I chased after strategies, one after another, from books, programs, courses, coaches, events, all possibilities, while my inner world was drained, exhausted, frustrated and resentful. There was a program that kept playing over and over … driving me.

I remember one day, driving home from work. Once again, I was tired, frustrated, juggling between multiple jobs, trying to build a business. Four years of grinding, and yet the results felt so small. I asked myself; *'Is this really what it means to thrive?'* I was doing more than I could give. I was pushing beyond my limits. I kept hearing the word 'thrive' in the personal development world, but I didn't understand what it truly meant … or how to live it. Now I know: *thriving* doesn't mean *more*. Thriving isn't just a word or a lifestyle, it is a state of being. It simply means *being*. More of you *being you* and becoming the version you're meant to be. Let me show you the difference from my perspective.

SURVIVING MEANS:

- Hustling and chasing
- Feeling never enough
- Living on default
- Pleasing others
- Overthinking everything
- Insecure, unsafe and overdoing
- Feeling anxious, overwhelmed or stuck

THRIVING MEANS:

- Feeling grounded, calm and clear
- Doing less but with more alignment
- Knowing who you are and your worth
- Choosing based on what *feels true to you*
- Living from peace, not pressure
- Presence over Performance
- Waking up with a deeper sense of self

WHAT DOES IT MEAN TO THRIVE?
Thriving isn't about perfection. For years, and maybe most of our lives, we've been moulded to aim for perfection, yet no one teaches us this. The reason we want to be perfect is that *we want to protect ourselves from being hurt again.* There is no final destination or some magical moment where everything is figured out. There is no *overnight oat process*, where you can wake up and '*be perfect.*'

I love this phrase, as I feel many people have this expectation, including myself. *Get it all done perfectly tonight, so I can eat it in the morning.* But it just reminds me that thriving is not a quick process. I was expecting it to be that way, until I realised that what I've built is not an *overnight oat* process. I've come to understand, that chasing and rushing are deeply tied to the feeling of losing time. And maybe, without even realising it, you're also protecting yourself from pain or trying to prove yourself to the world.

What timing in your life have you connected to a sense of loss, protection or proving? …when, in truth, it may be pointing you toward something meaningful.

This is the process of thriving; not a destination but an ongoing unfolding. You keep evolving, growing and flourishing through each season, each lesson, and each step toward where you are heading.

Pause here and ask yourself; *have you been building an overnight oat life or a life that's allowed to slowly flourish?*

If life is perfect, then surely it means you are at the final destination where there is no more progression. I was trying so hard to get to the destination, that I forgot to enjoy the journey. I so badly wanted 'success' to happen *the next day,* because I didn't want to be in *that painful situation* again. The more I chased, protected, performed, and proved, the more I was collapsing from the inside out.

Throughout this beautiful journey, I've come to understand and live in *a thriving state. Thriving is a state of being and becoming.* It's how you *feel* as you live, lead and love. It's when your inner world and outer world finally begin to match. When you're no longer forcing … but flowing. When you're no longer grinding, but grounding. When you're no longer chasing but centred, while attracting.

Which of those shifts, from forcing to flowing, grinding to grounding, chasing to centre-ing, would make the biggest difference in your life right now?

It's the moment you no longer live based on survival, but on intention, and allowing the true direction to take you. If you've been living in survival … you're not alone. You were trained to survive. *But you were born to thrive.* Thrive from the survival state of being and becoming the greater version of you. For me, thriving started with a shift. Not from the outside, but from the inside. When I stopped chasing strategies and started calming my body.

I've been chasing strategies, courses, programs, events, money, certifications and external validation, all to prove I was enough, I was qualified, I was capable. When I stopped proving and started trusting, when I stopped overthinking and started listening, that's when everything began to change. Thriving begins when you decide to live differently.

To move from:

- Outer Focus to Inner Focus
- Chaos and Chasing to Clarity with Order and True Direction
- Fear-based Doing to Self-aligned Being

Your story might be different from mine, but it is built from the same foundation and structure.

INTRODUCING THE MIND GPS: YOUR INNER COMPASS

There was a point in my journey where I knew something had to shift ... not just on the outside, but deep within me. I had tried everything. The books, the programs, the courses, the strategies. I was doing all the right things but still circling back to the same place. But for you, it could be different stories and journeys that brought you here. Maybe it's waking up every day to a job that no longer excites you, rebuilding life after a breakup, moving to a new city or country, or quietly carrying the weight of feeling lost, even when life looks 'fine' on the outside. The way you've lived it, the patterns you've followed, the rules you thought you had to play by - all of it has led you to this moment of *knowing something needs to change.*

It felt like no matter how hard I pushed, I wasn't getting closer to the life I truly wanted. I was surviving, grinding, hustling, pushing and forcing ... but I wasn't thriving. I kept asking myself, *Is there something wrong with me? What else can go wrong when I've tried everything?* I even wondered if the life that I was working so hard to build just wasn't for me. Every time I hit the wall and fell, I kept climbing back up to the same place. Over and over. But it felt heavier each time.

Maybe you've had a season like that too ... where you can't tell if you're actually moving forward or just running on the spot.

Through those deep and painful moments, I was trying to use an old system to navigate a new path. I was using outdated conditioning, beliefs, emotional patterns, and survival habits.

MIND GPS

Maybe you've felt like you were trying to move forward, but your mind kept using an old map.

I was running an old program, trying to build a new life. There was nothing wrong with me. What I really needed ... was a new internal operating system. One that helped me reset, recalibrate, realign, and reconnect to myself. One that understands not just what I want, but how I feel, how I think, how I respond, and how I truly operate.

If your mind could speak right now, what operating system would it say it's really running on?

That's when the Mind GPS was born - through the deepest painful moment. It gave me a new direction with a different view. I realised that the mind isn't just where your thoughts live, it's both the *gateway* and the *gatekeeper*. It's the gateway to your clarity, truth, potential and purpose ... but it's also the gatekeeper of your fears, doubts and old programming.

Which one feels more in charge for you right now? Your gateway or your gatekeeper?

It opens when it feels safe. It protects when it senses threat ... even when there is none. It can lead you forward or hold you back. That's why I needed a new system - not to fight my mind, but to work with it. To honour its protection but guide it gently toward alignment. Through the struggles, self-doubts, imposter syndrome and fears, over six years of building something I loved and believed in, this framework and method came to life. I was carrying it my whole life, in everything I did. It wasn't built from perfection. It was born from the chaos; from the real lived experience of breaking down and rebuilding. Of becoming more of who I truly am. Of choosing to keep showing up even when nothing made sense.

While I was on the journey of building my passion for work, trying to figure out how to turn something I love into something that matters, the Mind GPS emerged. It didn't come from reading a book or following someone else's method, it came from deep within, from listening to my breakdowns, sitting with the discomfort, studying my own mind and emotions, while helping others through theirs.

When was the last time you truly listened to what your *breakdown* was trying to teach you?

I broke down. I realised that our mind is not our enemy. It's our guidance system. It just needs to be understood and reconnected to. Sometimes, adversity comes to be your greatest gift. It may not look like a gift when you're in the middle of it, but now I see it was all leading me to this.

If you look back, can you see one challenge that hurts so much, that it actually might have been guiding you toward something better?

The wound becomes wisdom. The weakness becomes worth. The struggle becomes strength.

Reset, Recalibrate, Realign Your Mind GPS

Mind GPS is a whole complete system and framework I created through my personal transformation journey, and now, it's what I use to guide others. At its simplest, Mind GPS is your internal navigation system, your inner compass, that leads you toward your true direction. It's not about fixing yourself. It's about remembering yourself again and becoming who you're meant to be.

To navigate your Mind GPS, there are three stages you move through: Reset, Recalibrate, and Realign.

Awareness is the first key. Awareness is everything. Because you can't change what you can't see. When your awareness expands, your sky expands. You start to see further and wider. You begin to respond, instead of react. You start making conscious choices, instead of automatic ones. You begin to lead your life from the inside out. This is the moment where the Mind GPS begins to update. You go from being the passenger of your old programming to becoming the driver of your own direction. Just like a GPS needs recalibration to give you the best route, your mind needs these stages to guide you to your true destination. It's like when you're driving and take a wrong turn. Your GPS instantly says, *'Recalculating…'* and begins guiding you back on track. In the same way, recalibrating your mind updates your inner map, so you can navigate toward where you truly want to go.

In Mind GPS, each stage is more than just a step, it's a focused transformation:

Reset with Growth - Unlearn what you've learned. This is where you begin to release the old programming, beliefs and patterns that have kept you in survival mode.

Recalibrate with Presence - Lead yourself first, lead from within. This is about emotional awareness, nervous system regulation and learning how to respond instead of react.

Realign with Self - Step into alignment. You begin to live from your truth, embody who you really are, and move forward in the direction that feels true for you. *As simple as JKL.* (Something you'll discover in the coming chapters!)

Because once your GPS is aligned with your true self, every choice you make, every step you take, every mile you travel, starts naturally pulling you closer to the life you're meant to live. And here's the beautiful truth … reset, recalibration, and realign isn't the end of the journey, it's just the beginning. The magic starts the moment you begin to navigate, when you trust that updated GPS and let it guide you forward. That's when you stop just wishing for your destination and start living it … one aligned step at a time.

> *'Sometimes adversity comes to be your greatest gift. Thank it, Appreciate it, be Grateful for it.'*

SECTION 3
YOUR MIND GPS. YOUR PERSONALISED ROADMAP

Chapter 7
Your Growth

'Growth is not about adding more to be more ... Growth is unlearning what no longer serves you.'

RAISED BY STRUGGLE, PROGRAMMED TO HUSTLE

Growing up in a traditional family, culture and society, shaped who I was and what I knew, through learning from the roots of programming. I saw my parents working hard to support the family and raise children. I watched as my grandfather worked hard, until he was unable to walk, to still support his wife and child in his second marriage. He was a hardworking man and always reminded me *to work hard in life* to earn money. He had a business that sold cooking gas. In his old age, over 70 years old and barely able to walk, he still carried the minimum weight of the cylinder gas at 15kg each. If I saw him carrying the cylinders, I would help him lift the gas up onto his lorry or his tricycle, so he could deliver the gas. I remember the last time I saw him in person before I left for Australia. He made a joke – 'Work hard, make a lot of money, and share it with me.' He always reminded me to work hard when I saw him, but I didn't know that would be the last time.

My family was not a rich family … we had enough to survive. My dad was a hardworking man, and he did work really hard for his family. But as a young and growing person, I never understood back then, that I was only witnessing the struggles, battles and challenges of him living life just to survive. As previously mentioned, my mum always supported dad. She opened a small food stall, and a Tupperware business … and later, a cybercafe at the front of our house. Every moment of witnessing their struggles, has instilled into me a program; *that I need to work hard, so I don't have to struggle like them anymore.* All of those moments of struggle I witnessed, became programs in my belief system; the belief that I need to work hard, so I don't end up struggling. But ultimately, the message was, *no matter how hard I work, I will still struggle.* Back then, life was about surviving. That's all I saw and knew.

Throughout the growing, upbringing, witnessing, I only adopted the programs that led to working hard for money, just to survive. From these lived experiences, a belief was embedded: work hard just to survive. In my belief system, I understood that hard work is more appreciated than *easy* work. I used to believe that if life is too easy, you won't appreciate it. There is nothing wrong with that, however *the meaning I gave to 'an easy life,' unconsciously made me repeat through a system that burns me out.*

As I had seen it, working hard was the only way to success. Throughout my life, I've always had two or three jobs in one day. It makes me feel great to have many jobs. My body feels safe when I know I am secure in my work, knowing the income that I will receive is keeping me safe *from not having enough.* But I didn't realise this was a survival program, silently running the show; the program I adopted throughout my life. The truth is, I felt safe when I was working hard. If I wasn't doing enough, I didn't feel worthy. I didn't feel secure. Then one day, I came across a video that hit me deeply. It said, 'The hardest worker is not the richest person in the world.' Think about it, do you ever see the richest people as the ones working the hardest? That line struck me like lightning. It made me stop and question everything I believed about work, survival and success. For so long, I thought my struggle meant I wasn't doing enough. But maybe the struggle itself was the pattern keeping me trapped.

Maybe you've had that too ... doing something over and over, not because you love it, but because it feels like the only way to keep yourself safe.

When I understood this was something I had been operating from for so long, it all started to make sense. I could see the pattern clearly. And it made me wonder ... if we could see the hidden *code* that's been running our life, how different would our choices be?

THE PROGRAMS THAT SHAPED ME

As I began to unpack my mind to understand myself deeper, I discovered that working hard and working more *made me feel safe*. I love working, but doing so much, silently kills me ... softly and slowly. It shows up in everything I do in life. But I always feared what would happen if I stopped. The truth is, I was operating from a mind that was *doing more, to receive more. Doing more makes me feel safe and secure. Doing more makes me feel worth.* And I didn't even know it, but I was chasing safety, security, success and validation - and doing it all from a place of fear:

- Fear of not being *enough*
- Fear of going broke
- Fear of becoming a burden.

I was programmed to survive, not thrive. Doing more made me feel safe and secure; it made me feel worthy. And for the longest time, I didn't even realise it. What about you? *Do you notice a part of you that feels safe and secure when you're always doing, achieving or keeping busy?* If so, there might be an old program quietly steering your life without you even knowing it.

Growth Is Unlearning

Through my lived experiences, growth, to me, meant becoming more, achieving more, doing more, succeeding more. But real growth, I have since learned after hard lessons, is about unlearning:

- Unlearning the lies you believe about yourself
- Unlearning the habits that no longer serve you
- Unlearning the identities you wore just to feel safe and secure.

For me, growth started when I questioned *why I tied my worth to performance and productivity*:

- Why I feared rest
- Why I felt guilty when things felt too easy
- Why I needed to constantly prove myself.

It doesn't matter which stories you've been running or playing, you will find out these programs running in the background, based on what you saw when growing up. Everyone is running a different program, and that makes you who you are today. True growth, was when I realised I had the power to choose a new story. What I've learned has shaped me.

What about you? If you slowed down long enough to notice, what might you need to unlearn? And if you do let go of that old story, imagine what might change and what kind of person you would finally have the space to become.

The First Pillar in the Mind GPS: Growth

This is why the first direction in your Mind GPS is Growth. Because before you can reset, recalibrate, realign and redirect your life, your business, your career, your relationships or your future, you have to look at the operating system you're running on. You have to reset. And that starts with seeing what's been shaping you ... obviously, slowly or hidden until now. I had to clear space for the new settings. Here are a few questions for you to reflect on:

- Whose story am I still living?
- What have I learned that I need to unlearn?
- Is this true to me, or I was trying to protect myself?

These Roots of Programming became the foundation of my conditioning, even my identity. And they may be yours too. I want to say this gently to you, what you've learned, seen and experienced has shaped you *but it doesn't have to define you.*

> *'Yesterday may shape who you are today, but it doesn't define who you are tomorrow.'*

The choice is truly yours. Because you are the driver in your life, to the destination you choose. For all the struggle in life I went through, I am grateful, and thankful for all the lived experiences which made me who I am. Because without yesterday, there will be no today or tomorrow.

Neuroscientific and psychological research confirms this. Dr. Bruce Lipton, cell biologist and author of *The Biology of Belief*, found that 95% of our behaviour is driven by subconscious programming, most of which is formed by age seven. Dr. Joe Dispenza teaches that by the time we're adults, we're running on autopilot, repeating the same thoughts, actions and emotional reactions ... unless we can consciously interrupt them. According to the Hebbian theory in neuroscience, *neurons that fire together wire together,* meaning the more you repeat a thought or behaviour, the more ingrained it becomes. This is where the science of

Neuroplasticity helps us to understand, with proven evidence, that we are able to make the change from the inside out. Your brain and body create shortcuts; a system. That's why we repeat old cycles … not because we're lazy or broken, but because we're conditioned to survive in familiar ways; ways that protect us and help us feel safe and secure.

Breaking the Cycle: A New Definition of Growth

For me, the old way of growth meant achieving more, hustling harder, becoming someone *better*. But true growth, from my lived experience, is the opposite. It's about unlearning what no longer serves you. It's not about doing more, it's about coming home to who you really are … underneath all the programming. Growth is learning to take control of your life, be the driver of your decisions, and live more for who you meant to be.

I once thought success meant *never stopping*. Now, I know real growth begins when you pause, when you reflect, and when you ask, 'Is this path truly mine?' We often say, 'this is who I am' - and some may believe it's their job role that is their identity.

But what if who you've been, is just who you've learned to be?

I honour my past and I'm grateful for my roots; they taught me truth, strength and survival. But I no longer let them define my future. Now, every day in every way, I am learning and growing to be the best version of me, so I can live life that is meant for me.

How would you be able to break this cycle and create new growth and a new story?

> *'Sometimes, what we see and create is just to keep us safe … but what if the truth is trying to set you free?'*

Chapter 8
Your Presence

'The world tells you to perform. Your presence invites you to return.'

THE SILENT CODE BENEATH IT ALL

I remember a time when I was doing so much, jumping from job to job, creating content, serving others, attending coaching sessions, joining programs, showing up at events ... and squeezing life in between. I was still building the business while having two jobs on the side to support my living, while working out as an immigrant if this new home was for me.

I thought I was building my dream. But I wasn't truly in it. *I was performing it.* Doing so much for everyone and mainly chasing, without realising what I was doing.

Have you ever been so busy building a life ... that you forgot to actually live it?

My body was there pushing through but my mind was chaos. My presence? Gone. My mind was either worrying about the future or replaying the past. My body kept pushing through, without a break.

Even sleeping was still a race in my mind that kept going on and on. It's like your mind never switches off, running in the dark, instead of resting and restoring. I never knew this was slowly and silently breaking my mind and body down.

I didn't realise or even understand what *presence* meant. I kept switching tasks, jobs and roles, running here and there, chasing to build everything in life. But what's the cost of living like this? Not just for your body, but for your soul? I'd heard people talk about the Power of Now so many times, especially in the personal development space. I even bought Eckhart Tolle's *The Power of Now*. But truthfully, I never finished reading it. Not because I didn't want to … but because I was too busy chasing the *next thing*. Caught up in what I now know as *shiny object syndrome*, I kept jumping from one thing to another. My human operating system was stuck in a loop … to chase, to prove, to perform, to achieve because I didn't know how to stop.

What if the very system driving your success is also driving your burnout?

That was my reality. And until I could see the silent code beneath it all, I didn't know there was even another way to live. So, what is the *Power of Now*? I've heard this phrase so many times, but for years, it felt like just words; simple to say, impossible to live. It wasn't until I found stillness in the middle of my own chaos that I finally understood what it really meant.

I began doing meditation in 2019, for the first time, from Vishen Lakhiani, Mindvalley founder, through the *Be Extraordinary* online course. I didn't even know how to meditate, or what it meant, and at first, my mind kept racing - I didn't know how to stop.

Have you ever tried to 'be still' only to find your mind running even faster?

After a few years, I learned how to breathe from Niraj Naik, founder of SOMA breath, because I have shallow breathing, and sleep issues because of my breathing. I even went to a doctor and was sent to a breathing physiotherapist to check up on my breathing issues. Going through these experiences, I didn't realise how it has helped me to understand what *presence* is about. It's helped me to learn and teach myself to go deeper into me, to understand how my mind and body operate in real life.

For most of us, we think being present means just sitting still or meditating. But *presence is not just stillness. It's a pause. It is power.* It's being fully here, fully *you*, in this moment. Not who the world told you to be, not who you think you should be, but *who you actually are*. When was the last time you felt fully here, without your mind somewhere else? Presence for me is a deeper connection to yourself and the world around you. It's what you can bring from within and share with the world, without masks, chaos or uncertainty. It's in the energy you carry, the actions you take, the behaviours you choose, and the life you live.

Another question I've been asking myself for most of my lifetime - *how can one person's existence make a change in a world, just by being in their presence?* And what kind of presence do people feel when they are with you?

I've seen how one person's presence can affect and impact a family, an organisation, a community ... and even ripple out into the world. I've witnessed it in my own family, in the workplace, in the communities I've lived in. *It's everywhere once you start noticing.* That curiosity, that hunger to understand, has been my fuel. I developed a passion for exploring personal transformation, personal growth, the mind-body connection, quantum physics, metaphysics, neuroscience, psychology and timeless wisdom. And here's what I've learned: the whole world can't change for one person, but one person can change and create a difference ... to one family, one organisation, one community, one humanity and to the one world.

Through my own lived experiences, I've discovered that *presence* is the bridge between your inner world and your outer world. It is the action of being still inside and outside. It's where integrity lives and where your leadership is born. You cannot create real change in your life, your relationships or your work, unless you are first connected to yourself. And I call this Self Leadership; where you lead yourself first and you lead it from within.

Let me take you back to a moment.

When I was young, I was bullied. It started when I was seven years old. My dad was in the army, so we had to move several times. The final location we moved to before he left the army was back to my birth town. I started at a new school in Kuantan, Pahang, Malaysia. I don't remember much of that time, but I vividly remember one thing - as my introduction to the new school, I was bullied. There was a boy in my class who pulled up my skirt. I was so scared, I accidentally peed myself. I remember how scared and how unsafe I felt in the new environment. That experience planted something deep inside me; fear, shame, and a need to protect myself.

As I grew up, I felt different. I felt I didn't belong. I felt I wasn't accepted. I felt I wasn't loved for who I was. I was one of the tallest girls in school, weird maybe, and I felt awkward. At the age of fourteen, I began dressing like a boy - what people would call 'tomboy-ish.' I felt safe that way. But actually, it invited more bullying - not just at school, but also from society.

Another vivid bullying situation I went through, was around the same age while on a school bus. There were mostly boys on the bus. Every day, I was mocked, teased and bullied. I normally tried to keep quiet and silent in those situations. One day, I sat next to a girl friend of mine, and a group of boys kept knocking my head and laughing. I'd had enough. I stood up, turned around, and threw a punch at one of them. He hit me back, and I stumbled into the seat. I didn't cry. I just stayed silent … again. But the next day - I broke. I cried and begged my mom not to send me to school on the bus anymore. I had to go through it, until a few weeks later, when my mom decided she would drive me to school every day.

Reflecting on this throughout my life, it was normal for me ... staying silent, keeping myself safe, playing small and hiding. When I didn't take action or respond, it became a familiar feeling of being *safe*. But I didn't realise these experiences were writing the code of my subconscious, shaping my thoughts, feelings, beliefs, behaviours, on how I showed up in life; in every single behaviour and choice I make in my life.

Maybe you've felt that too. Maybe you avoid certain conversations. Maybe you say, 'it's fine,' when it's not. Maybe you disappear into busyness or keep the peace at the cost of your own voice. Whatever your version is, and though these patterns may have once kept you safe, they could now be quietly shaping how you think, feel and show up in life.

Over 15 years later, I am building my passion business, creating the life I've dreamed of, and wondering why it was so hard to make this life change. Throughout learning, I started to understand what was happening beneath the surface. I began studying the connection between my mind and body. The curiosity and passion led me to another answer I was looking for. That's when I read *The Body Keeps the Score* by Dr Bessel van der Kolk. He explains that the body stores unprocessed trauma. *The body remembers what the mind forgets.* Emotions and experiences, especially painful ones, get imprinted into our nervous system.

Another story, I learned through observing my grandmother. For all the time I knew her, she was a strong independent woman, always moving, always cooking and working for the family. Near the end of her life, after I moved to Australia, we could only speak on video calls. She had developed dementia. Every time we spoke, she would forget short-term things, but she always remembered and repeated the same stories; her painful childhood memories. My mom mentioned that every time they went for a visit, the same related stories were repeated every five minutes.

She spoke about the anger she held toward her family that had caused her emotional pain. She was mentally, emotionally and physically mistreated and that story was imprinted so deeply into her being, that even when everything else faded through dementia, *that pain* remained. It was stored in her body. It didn't surprise me. After understanding this deeply, it confirmed what I had learned. It reminded me that if we don't process our emotions and heal our wounds, we carry them forever. They don't disappear. They become the quiet lens we live through. That's when I realised:

Your body stores what your mind tries to forget. Your mind becomes the gatekeeper to how you live your life.

So, I learned throughout my lived experiences and observations, that *presence* is not just awareness of the moment, it is a reconnection to what's within. It is reclaiming your power, listening to your mind, feeling your body, knowing yourself and witnessing your own truth.

Dr Candace Pert, a neuroscientist and pharmacologist, discovered that emotions are stored in the body through neuropeptides; chemical messengers that affect our cells and tissues. This means that emotional memories are not just *mental*, they are embodied. Your pain, your anger, shame, your fears - they live inside of you until they're seen, felt and released. According to Dr Bessel van der Kolk, your lived experience impacts the brain and body, which will be stored in the body as a traumatic stress. This experience becomes a memory, not only for your brain to keep you safe, but also so that your body will protect you.

So, if you've ever felt like you're living but not really here, or like your body is going through the motions but your *self* is missing ... this could be the reason why. You're not broken. You've just been disconnected. And reconnection starts with presence. Not perfection. Not performance, not proving. But *presence*.

'Your mind may protect you, but only your presence can set you free.'

MIND GPS

Self-Leadership

Whether you're single, a parent, a worker, a student, a teacher, a manager, a team leader, an entrepreneur or whoever you are at this moment ... you are a leader. Not just to others ... but first and foremost to yourself. True leadership begins within. It's a about leading from your truth and continuously improving, not only for your own growth, but for the well-being of those around you.

Self-leadership is how you manage, direct and guide your internal navigation system; the system that decides how you think, feel and act each day. This is where the Mind GPS Energy Gauge comes in. It's a simple daily self check-in practice that helps you measure and understand your current state of being.

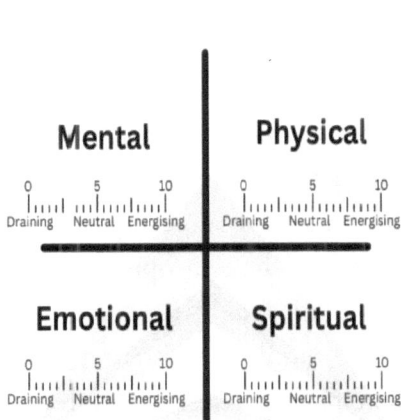

When you practice self-leadership, you are in the driver's seat of your life, not the passenger. You take charge of your internal navigation system – measuring, managing, directing, and steering it toward what truly matters. This begins with self-discovery and grows into self-mastery. Just like a GPS tells you if you're on course, your internal gauge tells you how you're showing up today. Your gauge acts as a simple self check-in tool.

Every day, pause and ask yourself: *Where am I right now?* On a scale of 0–10, with 0 being fully drained (depletion mode) and 10 being fully energised (inspiration mode), where would you place yourself? This quick awareness is your internal compass. It lets you see when you're on course, and when it's time to reset, recalibrate or realign.

You'll quickly see how your internal state impacts your external world. Just as one person's energy can lift one room, one family, one workplace, one community ... it can also drain it. This is why *presence* matters, not only for your own well-being, but for everyone you influence. If it helps to focus during your check-in, try adding gentle instrumental music in the background. Choose something without lyrics, so your mind stays clear. This can help you drop into *presence* more easily, tuning into how you feel without distraction.

The Art and Science of Listening Deeper

Through social media, general noise in the world, pressure in life and overloaded information - it's easy to get lost in the noise. When I was building my passion business, I poured my time, money and energy into so many places. Everyone had an opinion. Everyone was sharing, teaching and telling me what I 'should' do. Instead of clarity, I ended up more confused, pulled in a hundred different directions. Somewhere in that chaos, I learned something priceless; the power of listening. Presence isn't just about showing up, it's about tuning in, listening deeply, and being fully present with yourself, with others and with life itself. I used to think listening simply meant staying quiet while someone else spoke - but real listening goes far beyond silence. It's attention. It's energy. It's attunement. It's the moment you pause the noise, both outside and inside, long enough to hear what's truly being said ... and what's not being said at all.

Listening deeper is how I began to hear myself again; beneath the constant thoughts, the heavy feelings, the endless doing. Beneath the chaos, beneath the noise, there was a voice. My voice. The one that had been buried under years of people-pleasing, proving, performing, protecting, perfecting and paralysing. When I finally got quiet enough - I heard her. She remembered who I was. And here's what I realised; most people want to speak … but very few truly know how to listen, especially to themselves.

LISTENING DEEPER PRACTICE
Breathwork, meditation, yoga and being mindful are a good place to start practicing how to listen and quiet the mind. There are a lot of modalities shared these days. I share in my work, how doing simple conscious breathing, focusing your breath, will help you slow down your mind and shift states - switching between the brain wave states of beta, alpha and theta, to recalibrate your nervous system from a sympathetic state to a parasympathetic state. Dr Stephen Porges, founder of Polyvagal Theory, explains that our ability to connect deeply with ourselves and others, depends on whether our body feels safe. True presence begins when we listen, not just with our ears, but with our body, our heart, our breath. If you want to try conscious breathing, here's how:

1. Sit comfortably and breathe from your belly (diaphragm), letting it expand as you inhale and contract as you exhale.
2. Count backward from 60 to 1.
3. One count = one full breath cycle (inhale + exhale together count as '60,' then the next inhale + exhale is '59,' and so on).
4. Let go of all other thoughts for this moment, just be fully present with your breath.

If you want to deepen the experience, add slow instrumental music in the background. It can help boost your focus and presence, especially if you find it hard to quiet the mind at first.

PRESENCE OVER PERFORMANCE

Remember in Chapter 5, I shared the moment I was sitting alone at my desk ... papers scattered, tabs open, my mind racing like a Ferrari engine with no brakes. I was overwhelmed, leaping from one task to another, chasing the illusion of productivity. It looked like I was 'doing a lot,' but inside, I felt completely scattered and disconnected from myself.

Maybe you've had your own version of that moment - sitting at your desk, or in your car, or lying in bed at night, where your mind is so full, it's like every thought is shouting at once. You jump from one thing to the next, but never really *land* anywhere. You're in motion, but not in connection. We live in a world that worships performance and productivity; the hustle, the checklist, the constant doing. But no matter how much you do, if you're not present, you're not fully alive.

Our modern society often keeps us in high beta brainwaves, constantly running and locked in a state of high stress, the nervous system triggering fight, flight, freeze or fawn responses. But research shows that when we shift into alpha and theta states, our bodies and minds begin to regulate. We calm our mind and body, connect with our inner self, and access creativity and clarity; what I call the place of *creative creation*. According to a 2006 review by Cahn & Polich, during meditation and mindful states, EEG studies consistently show an increase in alpha and theta brainwaves. These states are associated with emotional resilience, introspection, and present-moment awareness. They are also the states where deep healing and rewiring can occur, what I call recalibration.

Dr. Joe Dispenza shares that, 'You can't create a new future from the emotions of the past.' That's because in survival mode (high beta), your mind is constantly scanning for threats ... not possibilities. It's only when you downshift that you can become truly present and creative.

If you could slow down your mental engine right now, what might you finally notice?

What would it feel like to create from a place of peace instead of pressure? Presence is not only the absence of action, it includes the fullness of being.

'Sometimes we focus too much on the outside, when the answers lie within.'

Chapter 9
Your Self

'Self isn't just a word. It's the root of everything, your choices, your voice, your dreams. Until you reconnect with it, nothing you build outside will ever feel like home.'

THE INVISIBLE MASK, THE INVISIBLE ME

My teenage years felt different; lighter than adulthood, with fewer responsibilities and nothing *big* to worry about. But that doesn't mean it wasn't real. For someone still learning how to live, it was everything. At that time, I didn't understand what life meant: no one teaches you that; no one sits you down to explain what life means. You just watch, feel, *absorb* and live it through experience.

For a long time, as I grew up, I used to hate my dad so much. Every time he came to the table for dinner, I would quietly disappear, just to avoid sitting with him. Being the eldest child, I had to be independent, responsible; that would often make me feel like the victim in my own eyes, a victim to my circumstances. My dad was a tempered person with a beautiful, loving heart, but he showed it differently. The truth is, I learned about his own childhood, his struggles, and how life had shaped him into someone strong on the outside but deeply loving on the inside. I didn't understand back then, but through it, I carried so much anger that made me rebel. Now that we are best friends, I see him differently. Talking to him as an adult, having a conversation and hearing his childhood stories, I understood where he came from. He is the strongest person on the outside, who wants to provide at his best for his family, and the most loving person I could ever see and feel on the inside. He was the fourth child out of seven. Life made him strong, guarded, always on edge. Nothing was allowed to go even slightly wrong from his point of view. As a teenager, I saw myself as the victim because of what I had to go through. But later, especially after doing all this deep work, I understood how these cycles have been repeating for generations. I realised he too had been through his own unhealed wounds. Later, I learned how these wounds and ways of survival aren't just personal, they're generational. Our patterns, beliefs, reactions are all passed down until someone decides to break the chain.

Growing up felt like I was enrolled in the *school of life* - that teaches, learns and stores the lessons I didn't yet know I'd use in the future. It has shaped me.

For much of my life, one of my most constant companions was fear. My mom, on the other hand, was my safe place. She shielded me from the world, spoke for me when I couldn't, and stood between me and anything that felt overwhelming. I couldn't even order my own food, I was too afraid to speak to strangers, unsure of what to say. I stayed behind her, shy, silent and hidden. What no one could see was the invisible mask I wore. I only became aware of it much later in life, when I started to understand what I'd been hiding behind; a calm, quiet face on the outside, while inside, my heart raced, my mind overthought, and my body braced for danger that wasn't there.

Have you ever worn a mask like that? Smiled when you were anxious, nodded when you wanted to run, acted 'fine' when you felt anything but? Somewhere around 2007, I was diagnosed with panic disorder. I was once sent to a psychiatrist because I couldn't control my anxiety. Back then, mental health wasn't openly discussed, especially in Asian culture. Back then, seeing a psychiatrist labelled you as 'crazy,' and I remember asking myself, *Am I crazy?* Deep down, I knew I wasn't. I was just struggling to breathe in a world that didn't understand. I didn't believe I was crazy, so I stopped going.

When I entered the working world, I wanted to earn money. I passed my first interview at a coffee chain but turned down the job, telling them I'd accepted another offer. The truth? The idea of meeting new people triggered my anxiety so deeply, I couldn't face it. No one knew. I just didn't want to face the social anxiety in a new environment. Around 2008, things had worsened and anxiety hit me repeatedly. I couldn't breathe. My breath would turn shallow, my chest would tighten, and I'd rush to the nearest open space, desperate for some air. My hands shook, my body trembled; I felt like I was underwater. I didn't have the words for it then; I just knew I needed to breathe. I couldn't understand why it was happening.

I kept going to Emergency at the hospital to see a doctor, but not for a physical injury. Physically, everything was perfect. They couldn't find anything wrong. Everything looked 'fine' but the cause of my symptoms could not be found. Some people laughed at me for visiting the doctor 'for nothing.' They didn't understand that 'nothing' was everything. The doctor even laughed and made some jokes to make me feel better because I kept coming back.

A kind, softly spoken doctor tried to help. He taught me to calm down by breathing into a paper bag when panic hit. That year, I began taking Xanax and Prozac. I clearly remember taking those pills that were helping me to calm down when I needed to. At first, it felt like relief. Then I realised taking those pills felt like I was still moving … but in slow motion. Like life was happening around me and I was just drifting through it. Floating and flying high into the sky. My body wanted to sink into sleep. My mind felt heavy, and even though the edges of my anxiety blurred, so did the colours of everything else. It was calm - but it was a numb kind of calm. The kind that makes you feel like you're watching your own life from the back seat. Over time, I asked those questions of myself; *What's the point of feeling this? I don't like this feeling! I don't want to rely on this*!

About a year later, I made a decision to no longer take the pills – I didn't want that to be my life. I knew I had to take control of myself rather than living with those pink and white pills. Later in life, when I began to study myself more deeply through my work, I realised something - my anxiety wasn't random; it was a pattern. A repetition. Every time I entered a new environment, my body would react as if it wasn't safe. I finally connected it back to my seven-year-old self - as I shared in the previous chapter; the child who felt unsafe when moving into a new environment, and growing up disconnected, unseen and unsure of *belonging*. That day, my body had learned; *new = not safe*. And years later, even as an adult, that old program still ran in the background, triggering anxiety every time I stepped into change and new environments. What I felt in my twenties wasn't just 'anxiety', it was my younger self's survival strategy repeating itself through my nervous system.

The invisible mask I wore wasn't just to hide from others, it was to protect myself. Unknowingly, it was my armour, my way of staying safe in a world that felt unpredictable. On the outside, I could seem calm and collected, but on the inside, I was bracing for impact, carrying fears I couldn't name, and navigating a storm no one else could see. That mask helped me survive back then … but it also kept me from being fully seen.

Breaking free didn't happen overnight. It started with realising that the mask had served its purpose - I didn't need it anymore. Taking it off doesn't happen in one dramatic moment. It happens piece by piece, breath by breath, choice by choice - allowing the world to see the real me. The truth is, the person you are under the mask is far stronger than the person you pretend to be. For years, I thought I was just *quiet* or *introverted*. I didn't realise the invisible mask I wore was actually a shield, not just from the world, but from the deep fear of being truly seen as myself. What I didn't know then was that behind that mask, anxiety was weaving itself into the fabric of my life, quietly shaping how I walked into rooms, how I spoke (or didn't), and how I saw myself. And like most disguises, it was so convincing that even I couldn't see what was really happening.

Self Reflection
Take a moment to think about your own *invisible mask*.

- When have you hidden parts of yourself to feel safe?
- What would happen if you showed more of the real you — even just to yourself?
- Can you remember a time when you felt unseen, and what story you told yourself because of it?

Maybe, like me, your mask kept you safe ... once. But what if it's now the very thing keeping you from the connection, opportunities, and the life you truly want? In the next part of my journey, I began to understand how these invisible masks don't just shape our personality, they shape our reality. They decide what we believe is possible, what we expect from life, and *how much we think we're worth*.

The Bigger You See, The Smaller You Think
Even after years in coffee shops, hospitality and other diverse work experiences that taught me how to connect with people, the quiet part of me, the part that wore the invisible mask, never fully disappeared. I

had built skills. I had experience. I had character. But sometimes, the old patterns waited quietly in the background for the right moment to reappear. In 2021, while building my coaching business and speaking career, I was given an opportunity to speak and spotlighted in a program. A chance to speak. To be seen. My body froze. My chest tightened. My breathing shallowed. The same invisible mask that once kept me safe as a child slipped back on ... only now it wasn't protecting me, it was holding me back. Opportunities would come and I'd find a reason to delay or avoid them. I told myself I needed more time, more practice, more confidence. But under that surface, my mind and body believed it still *wasn't safe to be seen*.

I realised I had fallen into what I now call the *Visible Worthiness Loop*; a hidden cycle where your worth feels tied to being visibly 'enough' in the eyes of others, so you keep waiting until you feel perfect before showing up. The problem? You never feel perfect enough. Even in workplace or personal development events, I was the quiet observer. I learned a lot - but spoke little. One small but telling moment happened during a Christmas promotional meeting at work. As part of a light-hearted recognition game, they gave out fun awards to different staff members.

Mine? '*The Underdog*.' The prize was a Cadbury hazelnut bar. At first, I didn't even understand what it meant. It wasn't until I asked a few colleagues later that I realised they saw me as the one who quietly worked in the background. This repeating pattern appears in how you show up.

Have you ever wondered what 'award' others might give you if they summed you up in a moment? Would it match how you see yourself?

Somewhere in 2019, I had written a vivid vision while journaling; I saw myself in a white shirt, standing on a stage, speaking to a huge audience. My heart wanted it. My vision was clear. But my reality said, 'How could this be, when I was hardly able to speak.' That's the thing! It's about how you think about yourself, in many ways. *To see bigger but be smaller in your thinking*. That turns into anxiety in mind and body so you can be protected and 'safe' again. Sometimes it's a fear of failure. Sometimes it's a fear of being seen. Sometimes it's perfectionism. Sometimes it's the deep, unspoken belief: *'If I'm truly seen as who I am now, I'll be rejected or not accepted.'*

The truth? My vision was right. In time, I did speak. At first, I spoke in small groups. I ran my own small facilitation group session and workshop. I coached people. And finally, I stood on a big stage at the Speaker Tribes Global Conference 2025 at Sea World Resort Gold Coast. Out of over 100 applications, only ten of us were chosen to deliver a 10-minute keynote speech at the conference. I was one of them. The mask didn't win that day.

Anxiety, protection, the way I think about myself hasn't always been my enemy. It was just an outdated safety strategy. *A vision you see ... bigger than who you are today ... might make you think and feel smaller.* But it is a sign - to move forward by taking one step at a time to become that version of you. Once I understood that, it became something I could work *with* instead of *hide from*. Through growing and evolving, one thing teaches me:

It is as simple as JKL - Just Be You, Know Yourself, Love Who You Are

And here's the question: What's one place in your life, right now, where your old 'safety' might actually be keeping you from being seen or heard?

As simple as JKL

It's a phrase that I hold on to in becoming who I was truly meant to be and shape how I now live my life to thrive. For so long, I drove my life with a mask of what I was told to be and shaped to be. That mask became my default setting - protecting, surviving, staying 'safe.' But when I started living using something *as simple as JKL*, everything changed.

No matter how big your dreams, goals, or positivity, if you don't connect to your true self, the journey can feel heavy, hard and exhausting. Have you ever felt like you're running toward something, but a part of you is quietly pulling the brakes?

That was me. I had big dreams, but my mind and body fought me every step of the way - fight, flight, fawn, freeze. Deep down, what I really needed was this:

- To be me again.
- To feel safe again.
- To come home to myself again.

Through knowing myself - who I was, who I am, and who I'm becoming - I discovered my passion, purpose, values, strengths, identity, dreams, beliefs, gifts, origin story, life timeline, experiences, weaknesses and wisdom. It was like finally seeing the whole picture of the jigsaw puzzle I'd been trying to solve my whole life.

This is the *essence of who we are. You are unique to you.* Irreplaceable. No one else is like you.

I started building my speaking confidence on small stages. For most of my life, I'd been my own biggest critic ... and my harshest judge. Have you ever noticed that sometimes the loudest voice telling you *'you can't'* is your own? I now speak on stages to hundreds of people.

The truth is, that voice calling loudly isn't the enemy. It can become your best ally - if you learn, know and love who you are. My mind and body weren't trying to destroy me, they were only trying to protect me, to keep me from getting hurt again. But being protected isn't the same as living. The more I connected to my true self - my essence, the real me - the more the path ahead began to become clear. I began to live the life I was meant to live.

J: Just Be You – Drop the mask. Be unapologetically you. The unique, unrepeatable you

K: Know Yourself – Understand yourself inside and out. Learn. Accept. Grow.

L: Love Who You Are – Embrace and love every part of you. You are already enough.

The roots of your programming shape you, but the deepest truth of who you are lives beneath the surface. *As simple as JKL,* you can live the life you're truly meant for.

Love is one of the highest emotional states you can live in. And when you love yourself, know yourself, and be yourself, you are living life at your highest level of feeling. You start to see the world differently - not as something you need to survive, but as something you get to fully experience. Wherever you are right now, can you identify it? Can you acknowledge it? And from there … can you start driving toward the better version of you? Because when you stop comparing yourself to others and finally start being you, something rises in you. Your confidence. Your self-esteem. Your trust in yourself. And that's when the real journey begins.

THE ROOTS AND THE REAL YOU

All this while, I thought I had to pretend with an invisible mask. I thought I had to perform to be enough. I thought I had to be perfect and change into someone else, so I wouldn't get hurt again. But the truth is … the deeper I connected with myself, the real me - the essence beneath all the programming - the more I came home.

That's the word. '*Home.*' When you don't know yourself, nothing feels like home. Not your job. Not your relationship. Not even the successes you've worked so hard for. Because deep down, it all feels like you're wearing someone else's clothes, living someone else's life. Have you ever felt that? Like you're showing up, but it's not really *you* that's living? In my room, I have a yin and yang symbol. It reminds me that to be whole, we must love and embrace both the light and the shadow. The highs and the lows. The strength and the softness. Everything has its place.

MIND GPS

When you learn to be whole, to love who you are, know yourself, just be you *and* choose to become the best version you can be every single day - you always progress. You're always better than yesterday. The deepest suffering doesn't come from failing, it comes from lying to yourself. From not seeing the truth of you. For years, I built my life on chasing, performing, proving, and perfecting, thinking that if I just did enough, *I'd finally feel worthy*. But I was building from a place of *not enough, not worthy, lack* and *scarcity*.

My real breakthrough came when I decided to stop hiding and start being. Start becoming. Now, I stand in my truth. No more pretending. No more comparing. Just me. And when the old thoughts creep in… when the mind tries to tell a new lie for me to believe… I remind myself to pause, listen, and return to my truth. Because remembering who you are really is *as simple as JKL*.

That's what I've learned about the self. It's not about becoming perfect, it's about becoming whole.

'You don't become yourself. You remember who you were before the world told you who to be. Because the deepest lie is the one you tell yourself.'

SECTION 4:
MASTERING YOU AND BECOME THE VICTORIOUS CREATOR

Chapter 10
Mastering the Inner Game

'You don't win the outer game until you master the inner game.'

THE GAME NO ONE TOLD YOU ABOUT

Earlier years in the journey of building my life, my dream, my passion for business and my life for better, I was running through all the things I could do to make it happen. I've run the programs and worked hard, as I've been seen and told to do. The ordinary pathway is to get into a school and university, get a good job, build a family, get a house, work for money and live life.

In my story to build my dream and business, I was still comparing myself to others. *Why does everything seem to work for them and not for me?* I never felt enough. I didn't even realise this was what I was feeling. I thought I needed more certificates, more learning and tools to help me reach where I wanted to be. I felt so small. *I'd been told and moulded to believe that, if you have nothing, no one will see you.* You've to be better, have more than others, to be seen. As a new learner at the time, I was looking at everyone on social media and what they were doing, thinking

I did not have what they had ... and that kept me chasing for more.

Are you chasing something outside of you, hoping it will finally make you feel enough?

I was looking at everything on the outside to help me move forward. Seeing what others were doing and what strategy I could use for myself. I always wondered why others were so successful and why I wasn't there yet.

As an example, I had a potential client who connected over Zoom and we met at an event where I shared my work at the Brisbane Convention Centre. She told me she had felt a shift after I was doing some mind work with her. I remember, she said, 'Wow... That was amazing... The music you played was speaking to me. I had been feeling *not enough* and anxious because of what I've been through in life, but now I see myself with power. Thank you, so much Amie.'

A few weeks later, we jumped onto a call, for a one session where we see what you bring from the unconscious, before the real work begins. I offered her a call to support her healing and transformation journey. On that call, she asked me one question:

'If you don't mind me asking, what qualifications do you have for the work you do?'

This reflection question from a potential client was highlighting my worth and all the mind stories I carried. Even though I'd been through a lot of change in myself, as well as seen and witnessed changes in others, along with all my qualifications, I still played the role of not enough and not deserving. This was reflecting back to me, making me shrink and feel small, even though it didn't show in my physical face. But deep inside, I was triggered by a simple question. I didn't fully understand what it meant internally but it hit something deep within me.

I was stubborn-headed, persistent ... and just kept going. The more I did, the more chaos I got into. I was so focused on looking and chasing externally. As I was reflecting back throughout my journey in the doing

… I realised I was wrong. I thought it was all about what I saw externally, but it was all played out in my inner game. What I was projecting out was reflecting back what I'd been playing inside.

No one had shown me, or told me, to look at how I *think, feel, and be* inside. What if the real work isn't about doing more but about seeing yourself clearly? *We've all been taught to see the external - only what can be seen through our physical eyes.* This whole journey has taught me how to look internally and it has changed the whole world for me. The lens I have now is flipped 360 on how I see, feel, be and act in real life and in any situation. The control that was once taken from me … has returned. I am finally feeling more empowered in myself and everything surrounding me. I have learned to be the driver in my life. I realised what we have within us is the power no one taught us how to use.

As mentioned earlier, Dr. Bruce Lipton's research shows that 95% of our behaviour is driven by the subconscious mind; a program formed from early life experiences. Most people are unknowingly *passengers* in their lives, living from old scripts. But neuroscience shows we can rewire these programs through conscious awareness and repetition. To take back the wheel. This is what it means to master the inner game. This needs to be taught to everyone to bring more goodness, love and light into life. We all see now that the world can easily be driven in the wrong direction. And this is the reason why I am sharing through my stories - to help you see what's driving you. To take your control back. To be the driver. And to truly live your life. Not driven by it but living from it.

Model of Reality

From all the lessons, I came up against wall after wall but kept coming back with persistence and resistance. I didn't know why I was stuck, why I sabotaged what I did, or why I couldn't get to where I wanted to be. But the more I dove inward, the more I realised this truth; my inner self was projecting into my outer world. And the outer world? It was simply reflecting back what I was unconsciously playing inside me.

You might be wondering how the inner and outer world relates to you. Well ... Have you ever felt like life kept handing you the same problems? Let me share with you a quick story of someone I know. She's always changing her employment because of 'workplace issues' ... but a similar situation happens again and again. Different place, different people, ... same story. I told her, 'it's not about changing your workplace, it's about changing what's inside of you that will change the situation.'

Maybe you have experienced that too - the same roadblocks, again and again. Whether it's in your career, relationships, or even just your internal struggles. That was me. Over and over. Until I started asking: *Where is this really coming from?* After all the life experiences I went through, the daily conversations, observations, and my deep curiosity and understanding of the mind and human behaviour, I came to one simple yet powerful understanding:

We don't just live in reality. We live in our model of reality.

It's the lens, the program, the filter through which we see everything. And here's what hit me: *How I think and feel shapes how I live.* My emotional state wasn't just my 'mood,' it was a signal. My thoughts weren't just random chatter, they were feedback.

I realised I wasn't just stuck because of the world 'out there,' I was stuck because of the program running inside. Most people don't even know they're running an unconscious set of patterns and beliefs formed by past experiences, cultural conditioning, generational passing down, and emotional memories. That internal model filters everything; your perception, behaviour and results. It's not 'life' that's holding you back. It's your current model of reality.

This realisation is what led me to create the Mind GPS 4P's Model; a simple but powerful way to understand how you're shaping your reality and how to shift it.

MIND GPS

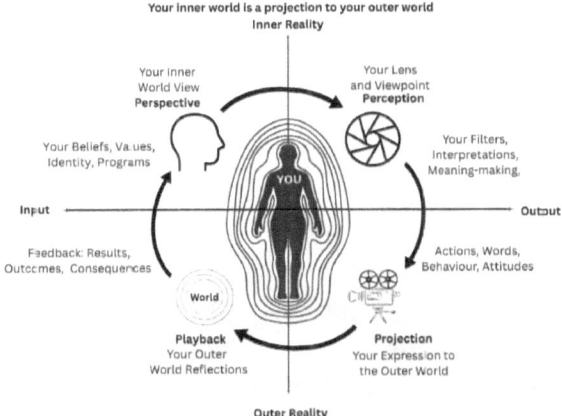

1. **Perspective** – The frame through which you see the world. It's your viewpoint, often shaped by past experiences, beliefs, identity, conditioning and programs.
2. **Perception** – How you interpret what you see. Two people can have the same experience but perceive it completely differently. This is the meaning you give it.
3. **Projection** – The outward expression of your inner state. What you believe, think and feel inside gets projected into your reality. Through your actions, words, behaviour and attitude.
4. **Playback** – The results and feedback loop. What life reflects back to you, based on your projection through your real life results, situations, outcomes and consequences.

Your reality is a playback of your internal model. Your perspective sets the tone. Your perception filters the experience. Your projection sends a signal into the world. And your playback becomes the reality you face again and again.

But here's the empowering truth. You can change any of the 4P's.

And when you do, you disrupt the loop and shift your reality. *And this begins within you.* Now that you see how your Perspective, Perception, Projection and Playback shape your reality, the first powerful step is simple: *awareness*. Most people try to change their life by controlling the outer world, forcing results, making more money, chasing success, fixing situations and changing other people. But lasting change doesn't start from the outside-in. It begins from the inside-out.

Ask yourself:

- What *lens* am I seeing life through right now? (Perspective)
- What *meaning* am I giving to what's happening? (Perception)
- What energy, thoughts, emotions, and actions am I putting out? (Projection)
- What is life showing me over and over again? (Playback)

Every experience is giving you feedback; an opportunity to see your inner model at work. Understanding this, allows you to become the driver of your life - no longer as a victim, but creating it. When you become aware of your 4P's, you're no longer stuck on autopilot. You can choose a new way of thinking, feeling, being and living. You can update your Mind GPS, and with it, navigate toward a reality that reflects who you truly are, not just who you've been conditioned to be. This is the power of self-leadership. And it starts now, with your next thought, your next feeling, your next choice.

Find Order in Chaos

What does 'chaos' even mean? For someone like me, with English as a second language, I had to process and comprehend it slowly to understand it deeply. It may be easier to explain with a simple story. I'm a person whose mind moves fast, sometimes too fast for me to even catch up. It keeps going non-stop, thinking about how to make things work for me and for my life. But I've had to slow it down in order to understand it better. There were sleepless nights when my mind kept racing, even while I was sleeping. That was really tough; many times I felt like I was crazy, that no one understood me. It was hard to live with the chaos inside my mind. It could jump and change in a split second. In real life, there were thousands of things to do, deep thoughts swirling, questions after questions, life lists, work lists, house lists, self lists … and all the lists you can list. It took me my whole lifetime to understand and realise this chaos I had in my mind was also reflecting in my actual reality.

One day I was coaching a client. She had a day off, and during our call, she said, 'Today is my day off, but I don't feel like I'm having a day off. I'm so tired. I tried to write a song, but it just doesn't flow.' I replied, 'Yes, you do have a day off … but your mind and body don't. Especially when your mind keeps going even while you're sleeping. Do you know it's like going on a holiday, but you're actually not on holiday?' She laughed, but it clicked for her. This conversation is to share with you how I used to live. Constantly *on*, even when I was supposed to rest. I know how it feels to live in that chaos.

That was one of the biggest lessons I've learned, how to truly switch my mind, to slow down, relax my mind and body, not just physically, but mentally and emotionally. Life, time … days keep moving, no matter what we do or don't do. But the real question is … how do you find order in chaos when life throws everything at you?

In my journey of building a life, a dream, and a passion business I've lived in chaos. Not just outer chaos, but mind chaos. Overwhelmed with information and too many situations. Not knowing what to do, or even how to take just one small step. I sabotaged myself and felt unorganised - mentally, emotionally and in real life. I've had moments when my brain just stopped, frozen in pain and overwhelm. Not once, but many times, I couldn't think, feel, or do anything. One day, sitting at my table. I put my head down, not out of defeat, but because everything was just *too much*. Too much to handle and deal with. I needed to pause. As I rested my head, I calmed my mind and body. I breathed into the present moment and put everything else to the side. I came back to this body, to this breath, felt everything I was carrying and … for a moment, I let it go. That moment taught me something powerful: *Even in chaos, you can find order.*

Everyone talks about meditation or mindfulness. Yes, those help, but when I first started in 2019, I didn't even know how to shut down my mind. I've had people tell me they couldn't meditate either, because the moment they tried, all their thoughts came rushing in. They'd think of what to do next, the problems, the lists. But this practice, over time, helped me find calm in the chaos. To be still in the storm of life. It's like the eye of a storm, where it's calm in the centre, even though everything else is spinning wildly around it. That's where I found clarity and calm. *Not by fixing everything, but by pausing. By breathing. By simply being in the now.* That pause grounded me. It reminded my mind and body that I am safe. That I am enough. And this tool is not just for your mind and body, it's for any moment in life. Any chaos. Because when you learn to pause, breathe, and be… you find order again.

Research from the American Psychological Association shows that mindfulness and breath-based practices can reduce activity in the brain's fear centre (the amygdala), helping to lower stress and improve focus. This is why just a few minutes of stillness can shift you from chaos to calm. It's not about controlling everything. It's about finding your centre again and again, no matter what's happening around you.

> *'If your mind is the operating system of your life, then your awareness is the key that unlocks its full potential. Choose to wake up. Choose to lead from within. Because the world you see… begins in you.'*

Chapter 11
Becoming the Victorious Creator

> *'A Victorious Creator isn't born from doing more, but from being and becoming more. When your presence meets your purpose, the life you're meant for begins to take shape. Not by accident, but by design.'*

THE SHIFT FROM PERFORMANCE TO PRESENCE

I spent years trying to earn my worth, to prove my success, but I did it without knowing it was my program that ran through me. Trying to be good enough, to be smart enough, to be successful enough, I wanted to have approval and validation for myself. *And to be seen as someone who has it all.* It was like watching a cute little cat playing, running and chasing their own tail.

Let me give you an example in one of my stories. Somewhere around 2020, I bought a MacBook for the first time in my life, the most exclusive and expensive laptop I'd ever bought for myself. I had been dreaming and wanting to buy a MacBook, for at least two years. I would regularly go to JB Hi-Fi, an electronics retailer, and loved to walk into the shop without buying anything, window shopping for the MacBook, touching it, visualising it would be mine soon. On the day 12 June 2020, I was finally able to buy my MacBook. I'd worked hard for it, saving the money for my dream. That night on my bed, I was opening the box, but I felt empty - a feeling I shouldn't have had after the hard work of saving for it. I looked at the MacBook and thought, *why don't I have any positive feeling towards you? You are right here in front of me.*

For a few days, I just sat with the question of why I didn't have any excitement about my achievement. Not because I wasn't happy about it, but I couldn't find the reason why I'd bought it. It was just something that I wanted to have, a desire that came from my programming. But I still couldn't work out why I wanted it. *Have you ever had this kind of feeling in life?* Doing something for your business, in work, in a relationship, but it still feels like something is missing? An empty or missing feeling that you maybe can't even explain. It wasn't until my MacBook truly helped me in daily life, being useful in what I wanted to build, making a huge difference in supporting me to build my passion business, that it now feels like I couldn't live without my Macbook. I started to see how this actually makes me *perceive life*.

Studies have shown that external achievements often create only short-term happiness. According to positive psychology research and Dr Seligman's 2011 book, *Flourish*, a new understanding of long-term fulfillment comes from positive emotions, engagement, relationship and meaning - not just achievement.

How does this relate to the life you are meant to live? Becoming a *Victorious Creator*, you have to know the purpose of being *you* in life; the reason why you are here in this world for yourself, and others. This reason comes from the inner core of being that will be part of your presence. The way you show up in life as your best version, for you and others. By being more of you in your presence, this will shift the way you present yourself in any situation - to yourself, to your family, to your work, to your society, to your humanity and to the world. You were to live ... not just to exist, but to truly live for the meaning of why you are here, that could impact yourself and others.

Through this, I learned to have *meaning* in every single thing I do. Because when I do know this deeply, no matter how hard your journey may be, it won't stop you. The winner is someone who finishes the race, not because they don't feel like giving up, but because they keep going with persistence, with faith and belief that something is waiting at the finish line. That journey is the most rewarding process of driving to the destination. Each mission marker or point of your journey is the celebration of becoming the *Victorious Creator*. Presence without purpose can feel empty ... but presence with purpose becomes powerful. That's when your actions feel aligned, not because of what you gain, but because of who you become and what you do with it.

Here's a reflection for you: *Have you ever reached a goal or bought something you longed for, only to feel underwhelmed or disconnected from it? What was really driving that desire? Was it presence or performance?* Or maybe you're experiencing it right now, having what you thought you wanted in life, but still feeling like something is missing or empty.

'True success isn't in what you achieve, but in how deeply you live. Presence with meaning turns achievement into fulfillment and that is the real victory.'

WHAT YOU BELIEVE, YOU RECEIVE.
For a long time, I did not believe in myself. Even if I had a dream and desire on my vision board, and kept telling people I was building my life, my dream, my future, what I wanted to do, I was often conflicted.

There is one person I met, with a beautiful heart, who saw me when I did not see myself. I met him in the coffee shop I worked at. I served him as a barista when he collected his Chai Latte most Sunday mornings. He was a very humble person, even though he was *somebody* in his work. He constantly traveled from country to country; somewhere new every time I chatted with him at the coffee shop. We became friends and chatted every time he came in. One day, I told him I wanted to write a book. I had a longing but it was just a dream without knowing how to achieve it. With his kindness and willingness, he suggested he might be able to guide me with ideas on how to write a book. One Sunday, in January 2023, I met him after work. As we sat and discussed book-writing possibilities, we got to know each other better. Knowing him from his story, I was honoured to sit at a table with him. How I appreciated this person who was willing to share his valuable knowledge and time with me. He told me: 'I am here giving you my time because I know, one day, you will help a lot of people. I believe and I know you will, since the day we connected at the coffee shop. That's why I invested this time for you.' *He made me feel seen when I did not see myself.*

Let's pause for a moment here. *Who is someone in your life that saw your potential before you did?* And more importantly, have you learned to see it for yourself yet?

For years, even though I had a big dream, I found it hard to believe in myself. I felt like someone who would often fail in life and business, and now, I was just making coffee and serving people. That's what I thought. For years, I didn't realise that what I believed, or didn't believe, about myself was shaping my brain, my choices and my life. That moment, sitting with someone who believed in me, became the moment when I learned to believe in myself, for the first time. The phrase I learned from Dr. Joe Dispenza, based on the Hebbian Theory and neuroscience's discovery, that *neurons that fire together wire together*, is called neuroplasticity. You are able to change through this process and rewire the pattern of your thinking, feeling and believing.

What belief could you be holding onto that is no longer serving the life you want to create?

Are you aware of it or not? If *yes*, are you ready to change it? In everyday human life, simply understand this, *you are the creator of your life, and it all starts in your mind.* As time went by, I realised that the way I think, feel, and be is what I *receive* in life. So many times, I tried to share my coaching program, I was rejected. Not because I don't know how to coach, but because I didn't feel *I was good enough to coach people.*

It showed in my physicality of not being seen as a confident person. That became a mirror, a reflection of what I received back, in what I do and how I show up. Have you ever been in a situation where what you believed about yourself silently shaped what you received - even if you didn't say a word out loud? Through this phrase, '*What You Believe is What You Receive*' I made an anchor for my direction as a *victorious creator*. A belief you stand in for yourself when no one else does. It's the foundation of a house before it's built, the invisible structure beneath your dream home. What you believe and not believe begins in the mind and shows up physically in reality. This is a true manifestation, not just wishing but aligning your beliefs, energy and action to receive.

I want you to know, you are the author of your book, the director of your movie, the architect of your building. The creator of the life you are meant for.

So, what kind of story do you believe and are you writing right now? And is it one you would be proud to live? To remind you, you have the control and power within you to make anything possible.

> '*Watch your thoughts, they become your words; watch your words, they become your actions; watch your actions, they become your habits; watch your habits, they become your character; watch your character, it becomes your destiny.*'

This quote, attributed to a number of philosophers, has simplified the whole understanding. This is the foundation of how you can be the creator of your life and where it begins. Right now, what thoughts have you been listening to the most? Are they building your life and your dream, or holding it back? I want you to observe what's in your thoughts and feelings that you may not be aware of. This model is created for you to simply understand how you can emit and attract from the inside out.

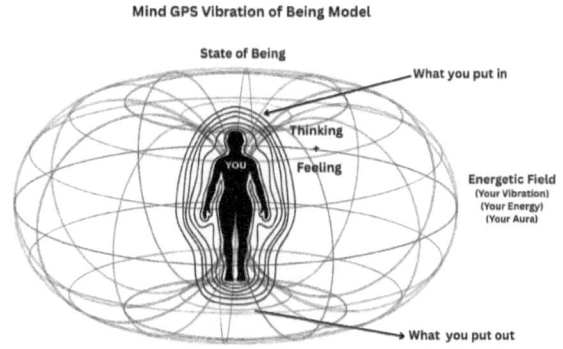

According to Dr. Caroline Leaf, a cognitive neuroscientist, every thought you think is a real physical structure in your brain. It releases chemicals and sends signals to your body, influencing your mood, decisions, and even your health. Thoughts are not invisible - they change your biology. I started to connect the dots. Emotions and thoughts are frequencies. And science now shows that every emotion you feel creates a measurable frequency in your body. That frequency directly impacts your nervous system, your energy, and how you show up in the world. According to research from the HeartMath Institute, emotions like stress, fear and anxiety create disorder in your heart's rhythm, leading to chaos in your nervous system. On the flip side, emotions like gratitude, love and peace create coherence, a state where your heart, brain, and body move in alignment and harmony. In this coherent state, your body enters clarity, calm, content and creativity - what I call a higher vibration of being.

Evolvance Strategy

Throughout my journey in pursuing my purpose, dreams and desires, I went through many challenges that could easily have pulled me away from my purpose. I came to realise that every challenge that comes in the way in life, pushes you up to the next level. This was also a test after test for me, that reminded me, *Do you really want this? Do you truly want what you think you want?* For me, my heart kept whispering and kept me moving forward. No matter how I fell, when nothing worked, when no one clapped for me, when nothing made sense, when distractions or roadblocks came along, I still worked towards my dreams. We can all easily become caught in victimhood, where we are reactive to life surrounding us. As a human being, our protective mechanism steps in, leading us to blame, complain, point, react, numb, freeze and survive.

This *Evolvance Strategy* came to me as a combination of the words *evolving* and *dance*; moving in the rhythm of life toward where I'm heading: *A thriving path*. I made a choice to grow and evolve from just being an ordinary person, working daily just to survive, into someone who created her life and rewrote her story. Through building the dream and living a life that inspired me to wake up every single day, I began to drive in a direction that was thriving, not just surviving. It taught me to dance in the rhythms of growing, of learning, of letting go, of rising again … for both myself and my life.

Have you ever been in a season where you tried to control the outcome, only to find yourself exhausted or stuck? That was me. I was someone who wanted to have control over the outcome to make it happen. When I started building a business in 2020, I didn't have a client who was ready to pay me. The expectation I placed on myself led me to huge frustration and desperation. I was still working two or three jobs while building it.

I was exhausted, ready to give up many times. Later, I realised the more I danced in the evolution of what I created for myself and my life, the more it helped me move with ease. One wise man I met said, 'Water flows with the least resistance.' That was exactly it! Allow the river to flow, and it will show you the way.

Neuroscience teaches us that cognitive flexibility, the ability to shift our thinking and adapt to change, is a key skill for well-being and growth. Studies show that when we resist reality, stress chemicals increase. But when we shift into acceptance and curiosity, our brain activates new creative pathways in the prefrontal cortex, helping us adapt and evolve. To support this, my mentor, the brain performance doctor from the US, who is on a purpose-filled mission with his work on brain rewiring, once shared with me a powerful insight about Neural Flexibility: *The brain naturally avoids pain and seeks pleasure.* But just like going to the gym to build physical strength, real growth often comes through discomfort. It's the tension in the training that strengthens your muscles - and it's the same with your mind. Mental resilience and flexibility grow when you lean into the discomfort, stretch beyond the familiar, and allow yourself to evolve … not by force, but by flow. Throughout the journey, heading toward a thriving pathway, this story, this dream I lived, this book, this work I am doing, it was where all of it was birthed into life.

Does this story relate to you in any situation of your life? Where you maybe pushed it through, tried to force it, tried to control something, rather than surrender to the flow of life? Even when something isn't working out, what if all of it was meant to happen for a reason?

What is every experience trying to show you? What if the obstacle was actually an invitation to listen, to learn, and to rise? This is where the practice of listening deeper comes in. Listen deeper for what and why the experience happened for you. Not just with your ears, but with your whole being. What if all of this actually wants to lift you higher than where you've been and where you are now? The only question is:

MIND GPS

Are you aware of it? Are you running with a victim lens - or seeing from a victorious lens? Are you just talking about it, or are you truly listening and witnessing the *evolvance* you're in?

I have a practice for seeing life differently; for shifting from reactivity to awareness. When something is going wrong or challenges appear, here is something you can use for yourself. I call it the Evolvance Strategy for real-life situations, challenges, or circumstances you face.

Finger Pointing Practice

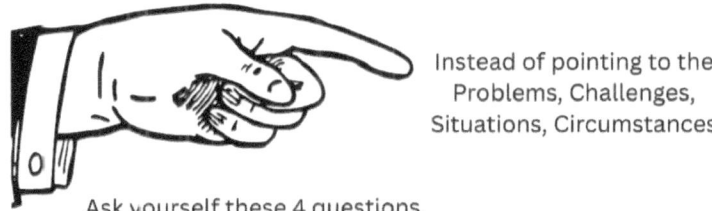

Instead of pointing to the Problems, Challenges, Situations, Circumstances

Ask yourself these 4 questions.

1. What is this trying to tell me?
2. What is the lesson here?
3. What should i truly see?
4. What am i taking from this?

This image above, shows that you are pointing your index finger outward at the problem, the situation, the challenges, the circumstances, or the person. But the other fingers? They are pointing back at you.

Mind Reflection: Next time life throws you a curveball ... Pause. Instead of pointing outward, ask yourself these four questions.

1. What is this experience trying to tell me?
2. What is the lesson here?
3. What should I truly see?
4. What am I taking from this?

Not to blame, but to reclaim your power. To stop being driven by your unconscious programming ... and start driving your life in your chosen direction.

ATTITUDE OF GRATITUDE

In anything I do in life, *gratitude* is one of the things that teaches and makes me see every angle beautifully. Being grateful was one of the things that opened my heart fully, with acknowledgment and acceptance. It helped me open another door of seeing the beauty in life. One day, I was coaching a client. I told her, 'Life is beautiful.' She replied, 'Amie … it's the first time I've heard that, I really don't know what it means.' I smiled and explained. 'Even when life is hard, you can still find something to be thankful for. Sometimes we forget the small things. But even the smallest things are a gift. For example, when you wake up in the morning, be thankful that you are still breathing. Be thankful for your bed, your pillow, the comfort that holds you through the night. Gratitude for these little things reminds us that life is beautiful. Because beauty is how you choose to see it.'

Still, she didn't figure it out until a couple sessions later. She went through the hustle, struggle and battles in life, as we all do. But remember, *life is a constant place for growth.* In anywhere and any situation, you can look to live a life with love and share it with others. She wants to live her dream life as a musician one day. To be where we want to be is not often a straight line. It's the journey we want to embrace and enjoy the most, in every part of it. At another of our sessions, some time later, she said, 'I understand now what you mean. I see life in a very different way now. Life actually helps me to see what I need to see. Now I see that life *is* beautiful. To enjoy every moment and grow from where I was.'

In any situation you are in your life right now or in future, *this attitude will help you to neutralise your state of being to an accepting and loving state of being.* This state will create peace rather than pressure. Love the moment, in any situation you are in. It's like being in love with someone, accepting both good and flaws, as whole and one. That is what true love is - when you have an attitude of gratitude. Look up the expansive states at Mind GPS: Emotional Energy Spectrum Model I shared with you in chapter 5. The emotion of love is up with the highest of vibrations to help you thrive in anything you do. And when you have this attitude, you will receive more in life instead of blocking it.

Gratitude practices can create new neural pathways and networks in the brain, making it easier to experience and process positive emotions. Gratitude doesn't just change how you feel, it literally changes how your brain responds. In neuroscience, the Reticular Activating System (RAS) acts like a filter, deciding which information from the outside world gets your attention. When you practice gratitude, you're essentially programming your RAS to scan for what's good, meaningful and aligned with what you value. Over time, your mind becomes better at spotting opportunities to see beauty and reasons to appreciate life. Not because the world has changed, but because your focus has.

Let me ask you...

What is one small thing today you can pause and truly appreciate even when life feels heavy?

How would your life feel different if you practiced gratitude? Not just when things go well, but especially when they don't.

MEASURE IT. MANAGE IT. MASTER IT
You can't master what you don't manage. You can't manage what you don't measure.

As a victorious creator, you must become aware, then intentional, then embodied in your creation. Your creation is what you are building and living who you truly meant to be.

Awareness is the key to create a change; awareness itself wins 50% of any battle. You cannot change what you cannot see. I spent years trying to do more, fix more, prove more, chase more. I didn't know that I did it, but the moment I asked myself, *What am I truly looking for in this life?*

What am I chasing for in building this dream? Why am I feeling scared to be seen? This was the first step of a victorious creator.

You *measure it with awareness, not judgement. Not to control but first to understand and then give compassion to it.* It changed the whole direction of how I navigated myself in making decisions and taking actions. It helped me to pause, understanding where my pinpoint is. I can see 'where I am' by identifying it. Measure where you are, compared to where you want to be. Writing it down will help you materialise your mind process outward and see it clearly. It will help you measure and see the gap. It's about noticing the patterns, recognising your state, and becoming conscious of what's driving you … moment to moment. And through that awareness, *then comes the choice of managing from what you've measured. And to master it, application through repetition is the next step.*

AWARENESS IS THE KEY
(as I repeat many times.)

Once you are aware, you can *manage with presence.* Not in a rigid and forceful way, but with presence and intention. In my own journey, I had to learn this the hard way. I was blindly navigating the direction I was travelling in, without seeing my destination. I wasn't managing my own mind and energy was leaking from it. I had to learn to manage it by honouring my rhythm.

You can manage your:

- *Energy* - not by hustling, but by honouring rest and flow.
- *Focus* - not by multitasking, but by choosing what matters.
- *Emotions* - not by suppressing but by feeling and moving through them.
- *Time* - not by packing your day. but moving in motion that nourishes you.

MIND GPS

And then *mastery with embodiment*. It's not about being perfect, it's about the embodiment of living through it. When you no longer dream about it, live it in how you think, feel, act and move. It is when your inner states create your outer reality. When you believe in yourself, it shows. When you have a vision and take an aligned action. When you no longer need proof and validation, because you already *are*. The mastery I've learnt is not about how much I achieved, but who I became through the process. The Victorious Creator is the master of their mind, not by controlling it, but by living in it and becoming it - by measuring it, managing it and mastering it.

Those who now lives in what you believe, walk with purpose and create from essence, not ego. And day by day, you no longer just hope things will change, *you become the change.*

> *'You don't need to do more to become powerful. You need to become more aware of what drives you, more intentional in how you show up, and more embodied in who you truly are. You were always meant for more. And now, you know where it begins ... within you.'*

Chapter 12
Envision Your Thriving Future

'You can't walk into a future you can't see. Before you can live a new reality, you must first allow yourself to see it.'

THE FOG BETWEEN YOU AND YOUR FUTURE

The way I was taught growing up, was to have success in a career, so it can sustain your future and give you a good life. As I moved through different fields, I was only thinking about how I could get enough money, monthly, to pay all expenses and bills, support the living life and earn more to have *what I want*. I only knew I had a big dream. But no one taught me about having *a vision*. I came to know that having a dream and vision are two different things.

What is the difference between dream and vision? A dream is a longing that you hold for a long time. But I always saw my vision in my head … as a vivid imagination. In an online course with one of Jay Shetty's programs in 2021, he mentioned that having a dream without an action

... is just a wish. But I still didn't understand the difference in vision. There was a moment when I was getting to know one of my colleagues in a coffee shop where we were worked.

Romi, a migrant, was a hardworking guy; a husband a dad to two children. He worked three jobs in a day. It reminded me how I used to be that kind of person; someone who worked *really hard* just to build a life and get money. Coffee shops normally begin early at 5.30am ... in the morning. He started his shift at 6am and I asked him ... 'how are you doing?' He told me he had finished work at 2am – so he'd only had two hours sleep. 'Wow ... You work crazy hard ... too hard.. don't forget to take care of yourself,' I said. But I had a curiosity to know more. The conversation continued every time we worked together. I asked him, 'Why are you working so hard, Romi?'

'I want to save money for myself and my family. I'm currently building a house in my hometown, and we want to bring our children to live with me and my wife in Australia.' I asked him if *he had a dream*. He replied, 'My dream is to build for my future. I want to work hard now and retire by the age 45, and provide all that my family needs.'

From all the conversations we had, I could see he was a caring husband wanting to provide for his family. One day, I said, 'I really think you need to get a good rest and some sleep ... it's ok to have money, but you need your health too.' He said, 'If I sleep I have a dream, but only if I wake up and get up, can I make the dream happen!'

We were laughing and joking, but actually, I heard what I needed to learn at the time - *a dream without action is just a wish.* I respected all his decisions for what he needed at that point in time; working so hard with very little rest. I laughed and agreed: 'You're right.'

Through many conversations with others, my favourite question is, *'What is your dream?'* This question itself will open to a deeper conversation I've had with many people. For me, I do have a dream; a big dream.

My dream has always been to be a motivational speaker, travel the world, become an author, run a business from anywhere, and everywhere, by having the freedom of time, money and location.

But still, this dream is just a dream without a plan, until aligned action is taken. But through my journey, I'd had enough of working hard to build a future. Yes, I understand a dream needs action and hard work to make it happen, but I need to change the meaning of working hard to *working smart*. When you're on the hamster wheel of continually running and doing, you get sick and tired, burnt out even, until you can find a way to make it easier.

So, through this journey, I learned not only how to build a dream, but to see the vision of how it can be. I've taken so many courses, programs, and studies to build knowledge and experience, while pushing through, because, honestly, I'd had enough of working so hard. I want to buy back my time for my family and loved ones, to do something I love, with fun and purpose. I'd had enough of running through a robotic life, going through motion for the sake of *working for money*. Yes, money is important, and I don't want to work against it - but I had to find a way to not kill myself with the same repeated cycles. There was a fog that blurred my vision to where I am heading. I didn't want to spend my lifetime, moving through to the end of life, just running a normal cycle, getting stuck in a job because you *have to, must do, should do*. So that dream I have, becomes a vision where I *see* my future. I don't know how it will happen, but I make it a vision of how I am going to live my future.

According to Dr. Tara Swart, from her work and her book *The Source*, when we visualise a particular event or situation in advance, we actually trick our brain into feeling familiar with the event. She shared that bringing together a physical and mental trigger will activate the body, as well as the brain, forming double the reinforcement for the desired outcome.

To give you some direction in building a life with vision … do you remember in an earlier chapter where I shared a story when I was at work and had a moment, a turning point in seeing the direction of my life? So … I am going to ask you the same question.

'Where are you now in your life? Is this a version of you that you are still expecting to see in the next ten years?' Let's go a little bit closer than ten years … I want you to envision three years from now.

How would you like to see yourself in the next three years? Vision it, see it clearly, you don't need to know how, just allow yourself to vision that dream without judgement and hesitation. Make sure it is aligned to what you deeply desire and, maybe secretly desire, if no one else knows about it. The vision that your heart and soul holds, not the one your mind tries to hold you in, with logic.

Close your eyes, open your heart, and fully see that version of you in the next three years. *Can you see it?* If not, what fog are you currently in that is blurring your future? Is this fog trying to hold you back from it? Well … let's move forward through it.

Vision Is a Frequency, Not Just a Plan

Have you ever written a New Year's resolution list, only to realise, months later, that nothing really changed? Or maybe you created a vision board to anchor your goals, but life still felt the same. For years, I didn't write anything down. My dreams lived in my head, floating like clouds without direction. Journaling wasn't my thing, until I discovered how freeing it felt to pour my thoughts onto paper. It gave my vision shape, structure and energy. It made me feel expressive, because throughout my previous life, I didn't know how to express myself.

There's one moment when I was traveling to an event with my coffee mentor. He wanted people to succeed in their dreams and passion. He knew I was in the coffee industry while building my dream. He asked me, 'Amie. What do you really want to do? What is your plan?' I answered him silently, in my mind; *I know I have a big dream and vision, but I have no plan at all on how to reach it.* He continued, 'you've got to have a plan, so you stay on track.' As he shared with me his business and future plan in coffee, he said, 'if you know where you're heading, you have to create a plan and work through it.' I listened carefully, syncing my brain to process what he said.

He asked me again: 'Tell me ... what is your dream? List it out for me.' I was processing, thinking deeper about his question. As I listened, I wrote down my list of what I wanted to answer him. He continued, 'Amie, dream big... you are so much more than what you've listed today. Think big ... but have a plan for it. What is your plan one year from now? Break it down so you can follow it through.' I listened, allowing his words to process in my mind. For someone who was a future oriented, visionary person, I was lacking in my follow-through process. I realised it was something I had to work on.

My vision became clearer, with a plan moving forward. I knew I wanted to be a speaker; so I learnt how to be a speaker from programs I enrolled in. I overcame all my fear and broke through my anxiety of being on stage. One day, the opportunity came up to speak on the conference stage. I made the decision to enter and was one of over 100 applications in the selection process. I made the submission of a one-minute video expressing and showcasing topics aligned to the conference theme. Before I applied, I could see the requirements and the types of topics they wanted to showcase. I asked myself, *what can I do to have the best chance of getting on that stage?* I was not randomly applying. I set my intention - and sent the application.

During the selection process, waiting for over a month to hear the result, I visualised myself receiving that email saying ... *Congratulations!* I was envisioning my future and how I was able to thrive in that future state. Every day, in my mind, I saw myself speaking on stage, but without any expectation; I was just seeing it as I expected to happen - in the toilet, while showering, while eating, while driving. BUT ... without putting any attachment and pressure on it ... just seeing and feeling it.

MIND GPS

On 3rd October 2024, around 7.15pm after my gym, I opened my email and received the email saying, *Congratulations you've been selected.* My hands and feet were shaking, tears were falling, and my mind was blown away with what was happening. I wondered, *Is this real, or am I dreaming?* I couldn't even drive the car for ten minutes ... it was unbelievable. No one knew what I was doing, I had kept it a secret throughout the process. What I was envisioning now had come to reality. You might be wondering, *could this even be true?* I used to wonder the same.

This isn't magic or wishful thinking, sitting on the couch hoping life will change. It's about shifting your *state of being,* so your mind, body and actions align with the future you're creating. When you raise your vision frequency by feeling, seeing, and living in that reality in your mind, you are training your brain and nervous system to believe it's possible. And when your inner state changes, your decisions, focus, and actions naturally follow. You start noticing opportunities you would have missed before, speaking up where you might have stayed silent, and taking steps that pull you toward that vision. That's why what once seemed *impossible* starts to feel natural ... and then, it shows up in your reality.

Why does this work? When you vividly imagine your desired future, your brain activates the same neural pathways as if you were already experiencing it in real life. This is called neuroplasticity, your brain's ability to rewire itself based on repeated thoughts and experiences. And this isn't just personal belief. Many neuroscientists have now proven that visualisation changes the brain. Brain imaging studies show that when you vividly imagine an action or outcome, your brain lights up in the same way as if you were *physically* doing it. Over time, this mental rehearsal strengthens those pathways, making your mind and body more ready to take aligned action when the real moment comes.

That's what I call *raising your vision frequency.* Your subconscious mind doesn't clearly distinguish between what's vividly imagined and what's physically happening. By *rehearsing* through envisioning your thriving future in detail, you condition your nervous system to feel safe, capable, and ready for it. Over time, this influences your decisions, your energy, and the opportunities you notice, turning your vision into a lived reality.

This taught me that a dream is not only a dream if you take a clear direction. And vision is more than what you write on a paper, a vision board, or your phone wallpaper background. Here are some quick methods I'd like to share with you.

Mini Guide: How to Raise Your Vision Frequency

1. Breathe deeply with intention. Centre yourself and signal to your body that you are stepping into a focused, creative state.
2. Put some uplifting music in the background. Choose sounds that elevate your mood and make you feel expansive.
3. Close your eyes, open your heart and visualise your thriving future. See yourself living it as if it's happening right now.
4. Use all your senses. See it, hear it, smell it, sense it, taste it — breathe and live in it as if it's your present reality.
5. Even if your current reality doesn't show it yet… feel how it is to live in that envisioned future. Let your mind and body experience it fully now, so your actions naturally align to bring it to life.

Create Your Future Self

Since that day, I learned to envision my future and what my thriving future will look like. It's not trying to be perfect but the focus here is on progressing, a motion towards that creation, and how that future is unfolding from what you were creating. This is what I call a *creative creation*, and this comes from slowing down your brain waves from beta, alpha, to theta. This then increases your emotion high to your expansive states, in the frequency based on the feeling you broadcast. Beta is the state when you are in alert, focus and problem-solving mode. But to get into the creative state of Theta, you want to breathe and go deeper. In the coming section, I will share with how this can support the direction you are moving in.

So, for example, if you know the life you want to live, a business you want to have and a relationship you want to be in, see yourself in that future, with exactly as that future situation looks for you. You want to be in a mind and emotional space of calmness, creativity and high vibration. Now, instead of randomly or defaulting your life with lists of goals, why don't you learn to create how you want it to be, and importantly, *without any attachment to it*. Let's do a simple exercise in writing a letter from your future self.

"A Letter from Your Future Self"

Dear _____,

As I am writing this today, 3 years from now... I am living the life you created. Let me tell you what it looks and feels like...

_____

The Bridge Is You

The bridge from where you are now, to where you want to be ... *is you*. *Yes you.* Dr. Joe Dispenza says nothing changes until you change. This begins with you and within you. What I am sharing with you here is from my real-life experience and how I learned to bring my vision to life in a smarter way. The table below, has a combination of my synthesis tools that align insights from science, consciousness research, language and lived human experience. I didn't invent this bridge, I simply studied, researched, compiled, organised them into a clear, and usable ladder for myself, and to share with you. This frequency ladder is like a radio station you choose to listen to when you drive a car. It plays the vibes of the moment and you listen to it, whether it is sad, happy, hype, or love. You simply choose which channel you want to listen to and vibe from it.

Frequency Ladder of Being

	State of Being	Language	Energy (Dr. Hawkins)	Inner Experience
Higher ↑	Being Mode	I Am …	Peace - Unity	Stillness, Prensence, Unity
	Aligned Mode	I Love …	Love - Joy	Flow, Joy, Purpose, Expansion
	Empowered Mode	I Choose …	Willing - Accept	Empowerment, Clarity, Freedom
	Awakening Mode	I Want …	Courage - Neutral	Curiosity, Hope, Readiness, Shift
	Guilt Mode	I Should …	Guilt - Desire	Tension, Anxiety, Judgement, Duty
	Force Mode	I Must …	Desire - Pride	Pushing, Proving, Stess, Resistance
Lower ↓	Survival Mode	I Have …	Fear - Shame	Pressure, Fear, Powerless, Stuck

Now, I'd like to invite you to use some real-life examples. Let's do this with your daily job.

Do you have to, choose to, or love to be in the job you do to earn money?
Do you feel any tension or pressure or are you enjoying it?
What about planning for a trip or holiday?
Do you feel you have to, choose to or love to?

Can you see how these different states of being create, your thinking and feeling? This connection from your state of being, creates the connection with your work and your holiday. Mood and vibes change just by seeing between these two examples. Now see what language you use in your day-to-day life.

MIND GPS

For me, getting out of my comfort zone, being on stage, and doing something new became something I chose and loved, even when I was anxious and nervous.

> *'Your thriving future doesn't start when everything is perfect. It begins the moment you decide to believe in something more. What is the life that only you can live, but have been postponing?'*

Chapter 13
Living Your True Potential

'You were never meant to shrink yourself to fit a version of life that doesn't light you up. You're here to grow into the fullness of who you truly are. One brave step at a time.'

YOU'RE NOT HERE TO BE SMALL AND PERFECT

By now, you may have learnt from some of my stories, what I went through to get out of the mind system that kept pulling me away from where I am meant to be. What I wanted to create was bigger than who I thought I was, as a human being experiencing life. I wanted to be that person I saw in my future, who I dreamed of … but I kept running away from it. No matter how much my mind told me to *'let go, let's do this!'* and I wanted to create and be it, I was still stuck in doubts, fear, inaction, procrastination, paralysis. I felt it was not for me, that I didn't deserve it. Because in reality, I had never been to that place. *It was place of unknown that created tension in my mind and body.*

I was a person who always procrastinated in what I did. In life, in any situation where I was scared, I would procrastinate, because in my subconscious *I felt it was better not to know the result or situation.* As an example, I created a masterclass to share with people about *Turning Passion into Prosperity.* Ironically, this masterclass was intended to help people take action, but in the beginning, I would delay posting it or sharing it (not taking action) because I had a fear of people not showing up. True enough, no one showed up ... because my behaviour was not aligned with my feelings. *It reinforced what I thought.* My thoughts became my reality.

Yes, it held me back many times; for not seeing my worth, wondering if I was able to do it – questioning; *Who am I to do all of this?* But I can break through ... understanding my internal navigation system, my thinking pattern, my feelings, and where my mind wants to go, even if my body is not ready for it. I could only remember what I knew from life I had already experienced.

Learning to play small and be perfect was something I built through a wall of protection, so I wouldn't be hurt (or hated) again. This is where I want to show you the layers I discovered in myself. The parts of me that were formed over time to keep me safe. Here is a simple visual of self-identity layers:

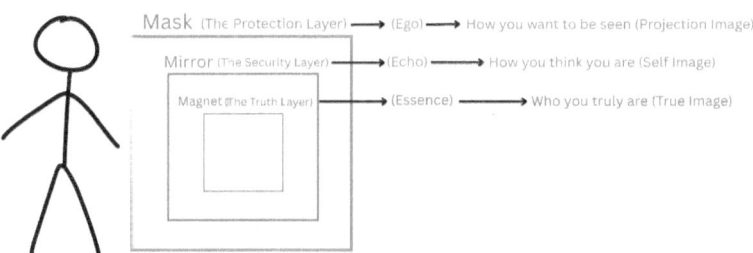

The Mask: This is the protection layer. Who I thought I needed to be in the world so I wouldn't be judged or rejected. It's the ego of how I wanted to be seen. I wore this version of myself to gain approval, to fit in, to avoid pain.

The Mirror: This is the security layer. The echo of how I saw myself based on the roots of programming. It's the image created of who I believed I was, built from feedback, beliefs, and stories I created for myself and from others.

The Magnet: This is the truth layer. The essence of who I really am underneath it all. The version of me that's connected to truth, love, and creativity. The real me, without the filters.

You might be wearing a mask too. You might be living from the mirror image of yourself rather than the magnet of your truth. And it's okay, we all do.

But *the moment you begin to see it; you begin to free it.*

There's nothing wrong with each layer, it served a purpose, they were built to protect you. *But what if you could now choose to integrate them, not from fear, but from your potential?* What if these very layers become the foundation of your becoming?

Adopt the Beginner's Mind

Sometimes, the mind protects us by clinging to what's logical and analytical; what's familiar. But what if thriving, the life you're truly meant to live, is waiting on the other side of that protection? What if the truth of your potential is not in playing it safe, but in stepping into the unknown? That unknown is where the new story begins, not from your past, but from your own choice to create. Through living in it and out through it, I had to choose to be the driver of my mind, even when it kept trying to take me back to the old, safe way. It was not easy. It was challenging. But it reminded me that the direction I want to go isn't behind me. It's ahead. I want to create a new direction, a new story, and a new journey. One that I choose and design. And to do that, I had to return to the beginner's mind. The mindset of starting again, like a child learning to walk, one step at a time.

Why is this powerful? Because every small step you take to think, feel, or act differently builds a new neural pathway in your brain. And research in neuroplasticity proves that even after the age of 25, your brain still has the ability to rewire and grow. The brain isn't fixed. It's fluid. It changes through conscious action and repetition. You may have heard people say, *'This is just who I am.'* That 'I am' becomes a mental program, a set identity. But the truth is, you can evolve through it.

You get to decide: *Do I want to stay in the same patterns? Or am I ready to build new ones?*

For me, I had to learn to feel safe by saying that *I'm not perfect* and I used to try so hard to be 'perfect.' But I choose to learn and grow every day to become the best version of me. Loving me as I am and growing. This is *as simple as JKL* and will help you move through it. In addition to that, I surround myself with environments that support my growth. I lean into people who reflect the higher version of me. I become my own loving guide, practicing what I call *self-parenting*. Because inside, there is still a child, your younger self, who may be longing for the love, the validation, or the worth that was once missing. And when you begin to change, that child might act out or resist, not because you're doing it wrong, but because it's unfamiliar. That's okay. That's part of the process.

Just pause. Be kind. Be patient.

If you can become aware and acknowledge that inner child, if you can offer compassion and love, if you can hold space as you learn something new, then you're practicing the true essence of the beginner's mind. It's not a weakness. It's wisdom. It's how we start again and finally become who we were always meant to be.

TRUSTFALL MIND:
Along my journey, I had to learn to *believe* in myself. But not only that, I had to learn to surrender my need to control the outcome. As I once

shared through my simple overnight oat process, I wanted everything in life to be certain, to be confirmed, to be assured. Because if I could control it, *(I believed)* - *I could guarantee the result.*

But real life taught me something else entirely; there is no certainty.

I used to think, *if it's under my control, it will be within my expectations.* And yet ... those very expectations often led to the deepest frustrations. I used to hear people say, *'Trust and Surrender.'* Silently, I wondered, *'How? What does that even mean? What steps can I take?'* Trust and surrender sounded abstract ... I didn't even know how to do it. I asked myself again and again. *How do I surrender?*

Where in your life right now do you keep asking *HOW*? Where do you feel the pull to control the outcome instead of trusting the process? I continued to question until I began to see it in action. Because the truth is, the moment you begin to question, you plant hesitation. *And hesitation, when repeated, becomes resistance.* Trust doesn't mean doing nothing. It means doing everything you can with full presence ... and then letting go of the outcome.

It's like the river that flows with the least resistance. Not because it's weak, but because it's wise. This kind of learning wasn't easy for me. As someone who found safety in control, the idea of surrender felt terrifying. But then came real life and real decisions. At one point, I chose to let go of multiple jobs, so I could finally focus on building my business. Before that, I used to constantly say, *'I just don't have the time to build what I want.'* And it was true - because I believed it!

I'd work long hours, and by the time I came home, my energy was already drained. Eventually, I realised I couldn't keep living in that cycle. Yes, I wanted to feel financially secure. Yes, I needed to support myself and make my family proud and happy, but deep down, I knew I was staying in the familiar comfort of survival. Staying in something just because it felt *safe*, not because it felt *aligned*.

What are you holding onto right now because it feels safe, even if it no

MIND GPS

longer feels aligned? What might open up for you if you loosened your grip?

So, I made a decision. And once I did, a thousand questions filled my mind: *What if I don't make enough? What if I can't survive? How can I pay my bills?* These were the real tests. And they came to see if I was truly ready to live in courage, love and faith ... not just in fear. Because yes, having many jobs gave me money, but it was my survival self, living in lack, running the show. It wasn't my true self. I knew if I stayed on the same track, nothing would change. I had been driving the same road for too long.

I didn't quit everything blindly. I made a plan. I listened. I went through the deepest fear of not having it all, and building safety in the real situation of nothing else is there. And through that process, I began building something deeper, what I now call the *Trustfall Mind*. This is where neuroscience meets the sacred. When you release control, you engage your prefrontal cortex; the part of the brain responsible for planning, visioning, and creative thinking. You literally begin to open yourself to more possibilities. New neural pathways form. Fear steps back. Imagination steps forward. *If fear stepped back in your life today, what would be the very first step you'd take toward the life you're meant for?*

Through this, I began to truly understand. *The Trustfall Mind* is taking action with belief, not hesitation. It is leaning into faith while still moving with aligned action, even when nothing shows up. It is doing something you love with courage, not staying stuck or surviving just to be safe. *It is the moment when control is released ... and alignment leads.* To thrive in what you're meant to be, you must go through a refining process, like the pressure that creates a diamond. This is what science calls a *perturbation process*, the transformation under tension that gives birth to brilliance. The strongest materials in the world are formed this way. *Where in your life is the pressure right now?* And if you chose to see it as the making of your diamond, how would you show up differently?

What if where you are now is just a decision to choose protection and be safe without falling? Are you ok living the same life for the foreseeable future?

The moment you choose the Trustfall Mind, you begin living the life you're meant for. And in that moment, you begin tapping into the untapped potential already within you.

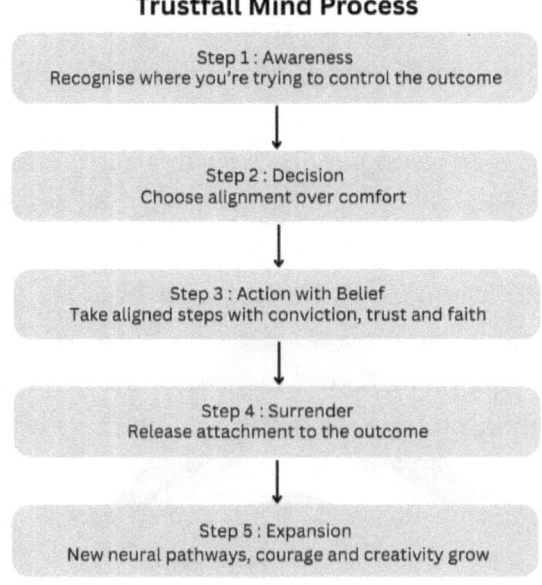

'Trust that life will catch you ... not crush you.'

Your Gifts Are the Gateway to Impact

In my stories, journey and experiences, the gift that came was wisdom. I'm certain your journey and your stories carry gifts too, even if they are still waiting to be discovered, explored or embraced. If you think about every superhero's story, none of them became heroes without a journey. They didn't just wake up one day with powers and purpose. They had to go through adversity, the trials that shaped their strength. They had to fall before they could rise. And it was in that rise that their gift was revealed. So, if you've made it this far in this book, if you're still reading these words now, I know you're *not* someone who's meant to live an *ordinary life*. You're not here to simply wake up, go to a normal job, get paid, and live out days without passion or purpose. You felt it; you know somewhere deep inside, that there is more to this life. There is more in you.

You are meant to be someone ... to do something that matters.

Every story I've shared with you in this book wasn't just about me. They were mirrors, showing you what's possible inside you. They were reminders to take back what's yours - your direction, your potential, your power, your gift is already here. Waiting...

One day, my speaking coach was coaching me on speech delivery, stage speaking and story-showing. After hearing me express my work and voice, he asked, 'Amie, have you ever heard this quote?'

'Most men lead lives of quiet desperation and go to the grave with the song still in them.' ~ Unknown

I was catching each word by writing it down, to later find out what it truly meant. It is a beautiful quote that reminds me we all have potential in us. That every human being is born with a song inside them. A unique instrument to play. A song to create. Music to be listened to. A message meant to be heard, even if it's long after they're gone.

If you've been learning, experiencing and growing from life, why don't you share it with others? It could impact many to lead a better life. Impact doesn't need to be big, even the smallest gesture, as simple as a smile to a stranger, can have a huge impact. Just as a coffee can cheer up someone's day, and an ear can listen without judgement. A hand to a colleague can ease everyone's job. An honest compliment without agenda can bring a smile, as well as a 'Thank you' or words of appreciation.

If you were meant to bring joy or impact through the music and art of being you, then maybe this is your time to tune in. To pick up that instrument. To let it sing. That's what I wanted to leave with you in this book. So, I ask you now, from one soul to another. What were the instruments given to you, still waiting to be played? *What is the song still inside you that's waiting to be sung?*

REFLECTION: ACTIVATE YOUR TRUE POTENTIAL
Before you turn the page, take a moment. Breathe. Reflect. Let this chapter land.

1. What would I do differently if I believed I was meant for more?
2. Where in my life am I still trying to be 'perfect' instead of being present?
3. What story have I outgrown, and what new story am I ready to tell?
4. What gift have I been hiding that is ready to be expressed?
5. If I fully trusted life to catch me, what's one step I would take this week?

Marianne Williamson said, '*Our deepest fear is not that we are inadequate. Our deepest fear is that we are powerful beyond measure. It is our light, not our darkness, that most frightens us. We ask ourselves, Who am I to be brilliant, gorgeous, talented, and fabulous? Actually, who are you not to be? Your playing small doesn't serve the world. Now, it's time to step in. You are the one you've been waiting for.*'

> '*Your story is not over. Your voice matters. Your gift is real. Don't let it die with a song still inside you. Let it be heard, felt, and lived.*'

Chapter 14
Creating a Life of Impact and Meaning

'Your real impact doesn't come from the job title, the task, or the act, but from intention, the energy, and the authenticity you infuse into it.'

IMPACT ISN'T WHAT YOU DO, IT'S WHO YOU ARE

One morning, I woke up feeling flat. Low energy. Poor sleep. You know those mornings where you go through the motions, but your spark just isn't there? I got ready for work at the coffee shop, as usual. The morning rush was already in full swing - coffee machines hissing, beans grinding in a steady rhythm, and the warm, rich aroma of espresso filling the air. Some customers were there for the ritual, enjoying that slow first sip. Others needed caffeine just to keep their eyes open. I wasn't feeling particularly inspired, but that's the thing about life, even when you think you're just *getting through the day*, you might be touching lives in ways you don't even realise. That morning, a regular customer walked up to the window. As I was making his coffee. He leaned in and said, 'You know what, Amie, I was thinking about something you told me the other day, and it made me think....'

I couldn't even remember what I'd said, but clearly, it had landed somewhere deep for him. A few words, a simple exchange had shifted his perspective. My own mood started to lift. Later that same morning, another customer came in. While waiting for his coffee, we chatted as usual. Before leaving, he smiled and said, 'It's always good to talk to you. It made me feel so relieved. You just made my morning.'

Again, I felt it. That quiet ripple effect. Not because I'd done anything grand or planned, but because I'd simply been present in the moment. It reminded me of something I've always believed: *impact isn't about big gestures, it's about the energy you bring to even the smallest acts.*

When I trained my staff in the coffee shop we used to run, I would always tell them: *Your energy goes into the coffee you make.* I'd say, 'Do you know what espresso really means? It's the expression of the soul. The way you make that coffee is the way you express yourself. That expression ends up in someone's hands, in their cup, in their day.' I'd explain, 'It's just like cooking. When you cook with love and passion, the food tastes different. If you were the customer, would you want a cup of coffee made with love and care, or one made without it?'

Every single interaction in life is like handing someone a cup of coffee; a little piece of you goes with it. You might never know the ripple effect. Sometimes it's obvious, like when a customer tells you your words stuck with them. But sometimes you'll never see it at all, even though it's always there.

One of my favourite examples of this came from a woman who worked at the police headquarters near one of the coffee shops I used to work. Her job was heavy, busy, and you could see it in her face. Every time she walked in, her expression was cold and closed off. She rarely smiled. One day, I decided to make it my mission to see a 'smile' on her face. I started by greeting her warmly, asking how her day was, and finding small ways to connect. At first, she gave polite, short answers … and then … a faint smile. Eventually, she began to initiate conversations herself. Soon enough, she would walk in smiling before I even said a word. And I can tell you more stories just like that. You can make others feel comfortable in your presence by the way you interact with them.

That's *energy transfer in action*. Science calls it *emotional contagion*. Our emotions are contagious because of mirror neurons in the brain. Your tone, body language and presence can literally shift how someone else feels without a single word being spoken. Warmth invites warmth. Calm invites calm. You may experience this yourself in life - when someone walked into a room with an intense or angry energy. That energy changed the workplace environment. And you felt it, didn't you?

And that is the true essence of 'impact and meaning': *It's not about what you do, but who you are while you do it.*

You can make coffee, work behind a screen, lead a team, raise kids, or speak on a stage, but anywhere you are where your presence is absent, the moment is empty. When your presence is full, even the smallest act can carry extraordinary meaning. When you pour love, care, intention and authenticity into what you do, you're not just completing a task, you're offering a piece of yourself. And that is where true impact begins.

Let's reflect on that with another coffee analogy …. What does your espresso look like? Is it sour? Bitter? Or does it balance the flavour with the natural sweetness revealed in the coffee extraction - like handing the world a cup filled with your best essence. A cup so good it brings people back to you. What cup will you serve to the world today? And more importantly, who will you be while you serve it?

Make Meaning, Don't Just Chase Success

> '*I almost climbed a ladder to the top, only to realise it was leaning against the wrong wall.*'

If you've been reading since the first chapter, you'll know I didn't start this journey with a clear purpose or meaning for my work. I lived a life working for money and building an external life; the image, the achievements, the boxes ticked. What I didn't realise was how much I was missing the true meaning behind what I was doing. Yes, I wanted to make a change for myself and my family, but I never stopped to reflect deeply into *why* I do what I do. I've always given my best in anything I pursue, and I could excel in almost any field I committed to, but at one point, I found myself at a real-life intersection - a choice between two very different paths.

I remember walking with Abbey near Brisbane City Park one morning. We sat by the river, enjoying the stillness, watching small yachts drift by, breathing in the fresh air, and looking at the calm water. I turned to her and said, 'I am confused with my direction. I don't know which way to go.'

At the time, I was fully immersed in the coffee industry. I attended specialty coffee events, learned about coffee tasting, cupping, processing, roasting. I even took workshops to experience judging barista competitions. I connected with experts who could open doors for me. I dreamed of one day being on stage for the Barista Championships. Everything was lined up for me to walk that path. But I didn't. Why? Because deep down, I knew I had to discover what I really wanted and *why* I wanted it. Through that process, I realised something important - I loved being in coffee shops, but not for the coffee alone. What I truly loved was people. *Coffee was just the bridge that connected me to them.*

I loved the science of coffee from crop to cup, and the story behind each bean. But even more, I loved the conversations. I loved noticing how someone's mood shifted from the moment they walked in, to the moment they left. I loved understanding patterns, behaviours and what made people light up. My passion was not so much with the coffee, it was with *people*.

During that time, I was offered several opportunities. A promotion to a higher management position in a coffee chain, the chance to manage someone else's business, and the option to open my own coffee business again. All of it sounded like success, but I knew I didn't want to be trapped in the traditional grind of long hours and constant demands. I wanted to pour myself into what I loved most - the kind of work that gives energy, not just takes it. I had to ask myself, *Is this the life I really want to live ... again?*

And while each offer looked like success on paper, I kept asking:

Am I climbing the right ladder for me or just repeating the same cycle I worked so hard to leave?

That's when I realised there are two ladders in life.

On one side, there's the Achievement Ladder; titles, recognition and hitting goals, but often without a deeper sense of fulfillment. I could have climbed that ladder in the coffee world easily, even built my own business and earned well. *But would it take me where I truly wanted to go?*

On the other side, there's the Alignment Ladder; built on meaning, fulfillment and vitality. Success that doesn't just look good but also feels right. The one where every step is rooted in purpose and the life you actually want to live.

One day, I was on my phone, reading an email offering me an assistant manager position. A part of me wanted it - for the experience, the status, the growth. But my heart whispered, *This will take your time, energy, and focus away from the direction you truly want to go.*

I knew I could excel in it. I knew I could climb that ladder fast, but I also knew I didn't want to reach the top, only to find it was leaning against the wrong wall. It felt like it would have been a lot of 'lost time.' So, I made a choice. I decided I would not just chase a ladder that gave me success. I wanted the ladder that gave me *'aliveness,'* not just achievement. Fulfillment, not emptiness. Even though I couldn't see the entire roadmap, I chose to listen to my inner voice - the one that told me to choose what felt right, not just what looked right.

And that's how this story ties back to impact and meaning. The moment you're on the right ladder for *you*, you show up differently. Your presence changes. Your energy changes. And that's when your work, no matter what it is, begins to create a ripple effect in the lives of others.

So here's the question for you:

Are you climbing a ladder that truly matters to you, or just the one in front of you?

If you reached the top, would it bring you meaning ... or just another title and money in the bank?

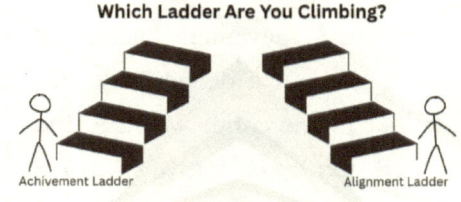

From my experience, success without meaning will eventually feel empty. But meaning will make even the smallest success feel alive. And when you're aligned, your presence becomes your greatest impact. Choosing the right ladder gave me alignment, but it was action that brought it to life. That's where the butterfly effect began for me.

BUTTERFLY EFFECTS : PURPOSE IS ACTIVATED THROUGH ACTION

After I chose not to climb the wrong ladder, I realised something important - clarity doesn't come before action. *It comes through action.* For so long, I thought I needed to figure out my whole purpose before I could take a single step. I waited for the *big vision,* the perfect plan, the full roadmap. But purpose isn't like a destination you can pin on GPS before leaving your driveway. Purpose reveals itself in motion. It's like the butterfly effect; the idea that a single flap of wings can set off a chain of events on the other side of the world. In life, the smallest actions we take can create ripples far beyond what we can see.

- A smile to a stranger
- A sentence you speak in conversation
- A choice to say 'yes' when you're scared
- A moment of honesty with yourself.

We tend to think impact only happens through big gestures; launching the business, writing the book, standing on the stage. But often, the real shifts happen quietly, through small consistent actions that compound over time. In my coffee shop days, customers would come back weeks later and repeat something I'd said to them in a 30-second conversation. I often didn't remember saying it - but for them, it stuck. It shifted something in their day, maybe even their life. That's the butterfly effect at work.

The same is true for your purpose. You won't always see the full ripple. You might not know whose life you've touched or what doors your small act has opened, but every action you take is like planting a seed; some sprout quickly, while others take years to grow.

Here's the part we forget; the butterfly effect works both ways. Inaction has ripples too. When you hold back your gifts, when you hide your voice, when you keep waiting for *the right moment*, someone out there misses the piece of you they needed. Purpose isn't only something you think about. It's something you live into. And you live into it by acting even when you don't feel ready.

You might not have the full plan, but you have a next step. Take it.

You might not see the impact, but you are creating it. Trust it.

Because the truth is, your impossible starts to turn into *I'm Possible* - the moment you stop waiting and start moving. Aligned action is the bridge. And sometimes, all it takes is the smallest flap of wings to change your world, and maybe someone else's, forever.

'Serve the world your best cup. Not just in what you do, but in who you are while doing it.'

Chapter 15
Impossible to I'm Possible

'Every great journey begins not when the road is clear, but when your heart says; It's time.'

THE ART OF BEING YOU

Being you is unique. No one else can do it. No one else has it. When I was growing up, I felt different - like I didn't fit in, wasn't accepted, wasn't loved or truly appreciated. As I stepped deeper into my passion and purpose, I felt it even more. There were days I wondered:

- *What if I'm crazy?*
- *What if I'm not meant to do what I feel called to do?*
- *Why doesn't anyone see me for who I really am?*

Maybe you've felt and thought it too - silently or secretly.

Most of the time, we try to fit into the world ... so it will accept us, love us and see us. Maybe not obviously, but subtly, we want to feel that way; *feel that we fit in*. And maybe sometimes, we just *do* it to survive.

To me, it felt like the world only valued the perfect, the impressive qualifications, the *right* job titles, the polished communication. It may even feel like you have to do more and be more ... to have more.

Me? I didn't have a fancy degree. English is my second language. I didn't have the *big* job that would instantly impress anyone in a room. Working in coffee shops, I often felt invisible. People judge by what you wear, where you work or the title on your name tag. But I remember thinking: *this job is just a role, a position ... IT'S NOT WHO I AM.*

I kept asking, *why does society only see value in what's on the surface? Why do we assume only those who 'have it all' can create something extraordinary?*

When I stepped into the coaching world, those feelings followed me. I still wondered if people would see my worth and my value. And then I realised, the real limitation wasn't other people's opinions, it was my own mindset; my programming.

I'd been comparing myself to others, questioning my worth, hesitating at every step. I used to live like that - holding back, scared of being judged for who I really was. I wasn't the same as others, but I knew one thing - I was living with truth and a pure heart. With time, I began to see that the journey was never meant to be *perfect*. It was never about getting it *right* from the start. It was about unfolding, layer by layer, into the truest version of myself. The value and worth I learnt to see, is not what's on the surface. It's the unshakeable confidence you have within you - knowing you are worthy, knowing you are valuable - just for being you. The deep core of being you ... is your worth.

This is the art of being you. No one else can be you. No one else has your exact story, your scars, *your magic*. Who you were yesterday shaped who you are today. It was your history - and tomorrow - is your new story. Every path you walked, even the ones that felt like detours or a long journey, prepared for this version of becoming you.

It may not be easy. Maybe no one understands you. Maybe you hold blame and resentment for why things happen for you. But I want to remind you, it was all there to shape you. So, walk bravely ... as yourself. Be proud of being you, even if no one else understands yet. Become your own biggest fan - not out of arrogance, but out of deep, unshakable confidence.

And remember... there are people watching you, quietly, secretly inspired, even if they never tell you. Keep being you, my friend. *The world needs it.* The reason I share this with you is because I had to learn through struggles, stumbles, and countless moments of doubt. I had to learn how to truly be me ... and to love me. That journey, with all its lessons and scars, is what I call *The Art of Being You.* Because the moment you stop trying to be someone else and start owning the masterpiece that is you ... you begin turning the 'impossible' into *I'm possible.*

YOUR REFLECTION:

1. Where in your life have you been wearing a 'role' that isn't the full truth of who you are?
2. What would shift if you stopped comparing yourself to others and started celebrating your own journey?
3. What is one thing you can do today to honour the art of being you?

MOVING FROM IMPOSSIBLE TO 'I'M POSSIBLE'
To be where I am today, writing this book - honestly, it still feels surreal. I never thought it would be possible. For the longest time, it was just a dream; the kind of dream *someone like me* could only imagine ... never live.

But here's what I've learned - anything in life becomes possible when you sit back into the driver's seat of your mind. You don't have to control every circumstance, but you do have to know how to navigate your thoughts, emotions, beliefs, and patterns so you can see the path clearly enough to walk it. Yes, there will be roadblocks, bumps and detours. I've had them all. *And every one of them tried to convince me to turn back.* I've faced self-doubt. I've felt like an imposter. I've been paralysed by fear. And I've been pulled back by the old stories in my head whispering, *You are not enough.*

One of the deepest stories came from my childhood. I grew up feeling unseen, especially by my parents. It wasn't that they didn't love me; they did. But as a child, I couldn't see their love through the lens of their struggles, responsibilities and unspoken battles. What I felt instead was:

I must not matter to the people who are most important to me.

As parents, they were doing the best they could with what they knew. They had their own burdens, shaped by their own upbringing. But as a child, of course, I didn't know that. All I could feel was the gap between what I wanted and what I received. And that gap becomes a story. And that story becomes the lens through which you see yourself and the world. A story you believe to be true.

That lens shaped my *Visibility Worthiness Loop*:

- I didn't feel seen, so I told myself I wasn't enough.
- That belief shaped how I showed up - smaller, quieter, holding parts of myself back.
- Others picked up on that energy, and I ended up with even less recognition or opportunity.
- This confirmed and reinforced my original belief … and so, the loop repeated.

Psychologists call this confirmation bias; the tendency to look for, notice, and remember things that match what we already believe. If you believe you're not worth being seen, your mind will focus on the moments that prove you right ... and ignore the ones that prove you wrong. Not because the other moments don't exist, but because *your brain is wired to filter reality through your beliefs.*

Here's the truth - the story wasn't reality. It was just the meaning my younger self made to survive. And as long as I believed that story, I couldn't see any different.

The shift came when I realised I had to *believe before I could see.*

Because once you start believing you are worthy of being seen, without proof, without permission ... everything changes. You walk differently. You speak differently. You choose differently. And the world responds to that.

What once felt impossible wasn't permanent, it was just a pattern. And patterns can be rewritten. The gap from impossible to *I'm possible* isn't about having everything figured out. It's about taking the next step, as if *you already are* the person you want to become.

One idea that inspired me on this journey came from Dr. Stephen Covey's *7 Habits of Highly Effective People*: '*Begin with the end in mind.*' Those words stayed with me. But through my own struggles and battles, I realised I needed more than just an *end* to aim for. I remember saying to myself, *I begin with the end in mind... but why doesn't it work?* I had to *align my mind* with it every day. That's when I created my signature quote and a truth that guides everything I do:

'Begin with the end in mind ... and align your mind to end it.'

Because vision alone isn't enough. It's when your thoughts, emotions, beliefs, and actions align with that vision. That's when what once felt impossible starts to unfold.

Your story might not be the same as mine. But I know you've had moments where you've thought:

- *Why me?*
- *Why does it feel like no one sees the real me?*
- *Why does it seem harder for me than for others?*

You're not invisible. You never were. The choice is yours now: You can keep waiting for proof before you believe … or you can believe it first and watch the proof appear.

Because once you see yourself differently, you can't unsee it. Once you believe you are *possible*, the road ahead changes. You start noticing doors you never saw before, opportunities you thought belonged to someone else, the right person appears in your life. There are moments where you finally feel at home in your own skin. That's how you turn the impossible to *I'm Possible*.

Reflection: Break Your Loop

1. Think of a time when you felt unseen, overlooked, or doubted
2. Write down the exact story you told yourself about why that happened. (*Example: I'm not good enough*, or *People like me don't get those opportunities.*)
3. Ask yourself: *Is this actually true … or is it just the lens I've been looking through?*
4. Write a new belief that supports the version of you who is *possible*
5. For the next seven days, actively look for even the smallest signs that your new belief is true
6. Each time you notice one, remind yourself: *This is how I break the loop.*

Your True Compass

There is one truth I want you to carry forward, the heartbeat of this entire book:

MIND GPS

Your mind is the GPS of your life.

When you reset, recalibrate, and realign it, you don't just find direction.

You create your thriving path.

This is more than a statement. It is a reminder. A compass. A truth you can return to again and again, no matter what season of life you walk into next.

You don't need another person's map. Maps are rigid. They tell you one fixed way, drawn by someone else, based on their life, not yours. But life isn't a straight highway. It bends. It throws storms. Roads close. Detours appear. And when you rely only on a map, you'll feel lost the moments when things don't go *as planned*. Your GPS is different. It resets, recalibrates, and realigns. No matter how many wrong turns you take, it whispers: *'Recalculating... this way.'* That's what your inner compass does. That's what your mind can do when you return to presence and realign with yourself.

The truth is, your compass has always been inside you. It's the small voice that says *'this way'* when the world is loud. It's the feeling in your chest that expands when you're aligned and tightens when you're not. It doesn't shout. It doesn't rush. It simply points north. And here's the best part; you don't need to see the whole road. A GPS never shows you every turn at once. It only gives you the next step. That's all you need — one step in alignment. Then another. And another. That's how you'll walk your path. Not someone else's. Yours.

You might be wondering: *'Why focus on the mind, Amie? Why not the body?'* Because the mind is the navigator. It filters your experiences, creates meaning, and directs your attention. It decides whether you see possibilities or problems. Your body is the vehicle. It carries the impact of your mind's choices. In the *Mind GPS* work, all three are included —

mind, body, and self. But the mind sets the route. The body carries you on the road. The self is the driver you're becoming along the way.

And the beginning of all this? *Awareness...* Awareness in the mind opens the rest of the journey. This is the importance of thriving by beginning with your internal navigation system. Your true compass is and has always been within you.

Your Journey Begins : A New Beginning

You've made it here. To the end of this book ... but really, this is just the beginning of something new. Because now, you can't unknow what you now know. You've seen how the mind works, how your beliefs shape your reality, how your body holds your stories, and how your inner GPS can guide you to the life you're meant for. You've read my stories ... but I didn't share them for you to admire my journey, I shared them so you could remember your own stories and discover where there are possibilities for you.

The truth is, there will never be a *perfect* time. Life won't line up the pieces neatly for you before you begin. Your mind will still have fears. The road ahead will still have turns you didn't expect. But you've already proven you can do hard things. You've already walked through fires you thought might burn you ... and yet, here you are.

So, this is where you take the next step. Not because it's safe. Not because it's guaranteed. But because your soul is whispering ... *it's time.* Time to stop waiting for permission. Time to stop climbing ladders that don't belong to you. Time to stop silencing the song inside you. And time to trust that when you leap, life will meet you ... not crush you.

A journey begins with one small step. Each day, little by little.

There's a Malay proverb that says:

'sikit-sikit.. lama-lama jadi bukit...'
— *little by little, each small step will build a mountain.*

MIND GPS

The meaning is simple: even the smallest effort, when repeated over time, will grow into something significant. The same truth applies to your journey. Knowing your destination gives you direction, but it's the small steps, the small wins, the small acts of faith that build the mountain of your life. Don't wait to celebrate only the *big* moments. Celebrate the small ones. They build mountains. They are what carry you forward.

As my mentor once said, 'Be faithful to the small, and the big will come.'

And here's why this matters - because you are not here to live on autopilot, to play small, or to repeat survival cycles. You are here to create, to grow, to live, to lead, to love, to impact - in your way, in your timing, in your truth.

So here's my invitation to you:

- Start before you're ready.
- Trust before you see.
- Live before you lose another day.

Your journey begins here. And you - exactly as you are right now - are ready. This is your moment. Not next week. Not when you feel *ready*. This moment right here is where your old story ends, and your new one begins.

"You are the driver now. Trust your Mind GPS and keep moving toward the life you're meant for."
Amie Radzi

www.ingramcontent.com/pod-product-compliance
Lightning Source LLC
Chambersburg PA
CBHW030327080526
44584CB00012B/753